D1121564

AFTER ONE-
HUNDRED-
AND-TWENTY

LIBRARY OF JEWISH IDEAS

Cosponsored by the Tikvah Fund

The series presents engaging and authoritative treatments of core
Jewish concepts in a form appealing to general readers who are curious
about Jewish treatments of key areas of human thought and experience.

AFTER ONE-HUNDRED-AND-TWENTY

REFLECTING ON DEATH, MOURNING, AND THE AFTERLIFE IN THE JEWISH TRADITION

HILLEL HALKIN

PRINCETON UNIVERSITY PRESS

Princeton and Oxford

Library of Congress Cataloging-in-Publication Data

Halkin, Hillel, 1939– author.

After one-hundred-and-twenty : reflecting on death, mourning,
and the afterlife in the Jewish tradition / Hillel Halkin.

pages cm. — (Library of Jewish ideas)

Includes bibliographical references.

ISBN 978-0-691-14974-5 (hardcover : alk. paper) — ISBN 0-691-
14974-7 (hardcover : alk. paper) 1. Death—Religious aspects—
Judaism. 2. Jewish mourning customs. I. Title. II. Title: After 120.

BM635.4.H35 2016

296.3'3—dc23

2015033172

British Library Cataloging-in-Publication Data is available

Publication of this book has been aided by the Tikvah Fund

Excerpts in Chapter 2 from *The Book of Legends/Sefer ha-
Aggadah: Legends from the Talmud and Midrash* by Hayyim
Nahman Bialik, copyright © 1992 by Schocken Books, a division
of Random House LLC. Used by permission of Schocken
Books, an imprint of the Knopf Doubleday Publishing Group, a
division of Penguin Random House LLC. All rights reserved.

This book has been composed in Serlio and Linux Libertine

Printed on acid-free paper. ∞

Printed in the United States of America

1 2 3 4 5 6 7 8 9 10

AFTER ONE-
HUNDRED-
AND-TWENTY

BY WAY OF AN INTRODUCTION

A FRIEND ASKED ME WHY I WANTED TO WRITE THIS BOOK and I said, "Well, they say death is a foreign country. At my age, it's time to start thinking about the travel arrangements."

"Good idea," he said. "If you don't like them, you can always go somewhere else."

Touché!

We joke about death for the same reasons that we joke about other frightening things. *Because* they are frightening. Because laughter is a defense against fear. Because it can be a victory over fear, a way of acknowledging fear's existence while demonstrating that it hasn't gotten the better of us.

But we also joke about death because, from a certain angle, it *is* funny. Nothing could be more preposterous. One minute you're a breathing, sentient being and the next you're a lump of senseless matter. It's the ultimate disappearing act: now I see you, now I don't. Even little babies laugh at that.

Except that they don't, not really. What babies laugh at is: now I see you, now I don't, *now I see you again.* A great deal of humankind's thinking about death has taken its cue from that.

And the potential humor in the *poof! it's gone* of a life is only there in a life already lived. A joke about the death of an elderly person that makes us laugh would be cruel if told about a young one.

As a boy, my fear of death was no joke. I remember exactly how it started. I was eleven or twelve, at home from school with a fever. By my bed was a copy of *Reader's Digest*. In it was an article about leprosy. This was, it turned out, a real disease that caused disfigurement and could kill you, not just a biblical affliction in the book of Leviticus that my class had studied in the Jewish school I attended. It sometimes started with white spots on the skin.

The next day I noticed a small white spot on the underside of my arm. I had leprosy. I would die.

I don't remember how long my leprosy lasted. In the end, the spot grew no larger, no new ones appeared, and it was clear that nothing was wrong with me.

But that was just the beginning. In the years to come, I contracted one fatal disease after another: polio, brain cancer, leukemia, multiple sclerosis, muscular dystrophy. One summer I had rabies after being nipped on a knuckle by a dog. Rabies, if you weren't immunized at once, was fatal. The incubation period was up to sixty days. For sixty days, I waited for the signs of it.

In retrospect, this, too, can seem funny. I've regaled friends with accounts of it. At the time, though, I lived with intermittent terror.

Intermittent jubilation as well: the jubilation of the sixty-first day. I would live! Life never seemed so bounteous, so luminously full of promise, as it did then.

The oddest part of it was that I never shared my fears with anyone. Had I told my parents, they might have looked at my nipped finger and either taken me to a doctor or told me to stop worrying. But that would have spoiled the game I was playing with death.

And it *was* a game, although it took me many years to understand that. I couldn't have said at the time what imagined threat or crime made me think I was living on death row; whatever it was, though, I sat in my cell expecting the knock to come. I could only escape death by outwitting it, which I did by tricking it into thinking it needn't trouble itself because I was already fatally stricken. I was playing dead like a mouse in the claws of a cat and doing it so well that I was fooled by my own ruse.

This went on for a while. It was my secret. Nothing about me gave it away. I was a top student in my New York public high school. I won track medals and literary prizes. I did the things that boys my age did and had the fun that boys my age had. No one could have guessed that I lay in bed at night praying for another year of the life I desperately craved.

Eventually, I outgrew it. Or rather, I traded my boyhood hypochondria for a more stable, long-term arrangement. I no longer had this or that fatal condition. The fatal condition was now simply being me. I was doomed to die young—if not this year, then the next or the year after that. At fifteen, I didn't think I would reach twenty. This, too, was apparently good enough for death, because it continued to leave me alone. Perhaps by then it had lost all interest in me.

I should have realized it had never had any in the first place. The summer I was nineteen, a friend and I bought a used car and drove it to Mexico City. Although I had only gotten my driver's license a week before setting out, this seemed no disqualification. And in fact, it was my friend, not I, who was driving when we had the accident.

We were on a mountainous stretch of a narrow, winding road quaintly called the Pan-American Highway. On one side was a sheer drop to a ravine far below. A light rain was falling As we started to skid, my friend had one hand on the wheel and was singing with his head halfway out the window. I was spreading mustard on a sandwich. The last thing I remember thinking before we plunged off the ravine side of the road into the single tree growing beside it was, "Damn, I wanted to eat this sandwich!" The tree stopped us with a jolt. The car was more banged up than we were.

If death had been looking for a chance to finish me off, it was more incompetent than I had imagined.

Yet even this did not quite convince me. The conclusion I drew was a different one. Death still had me in its sights. I just had, it now turned out, an ally that was protecting me, a private angel or daemon. As long as I kept faith with it, it would keep faith with me.

In one form or another, this belief stayed with me. Only in recent years have I lost it—perhaps because, betrayed by me too often, my daemon has departed, perhaps because I've ceased needing its protection. Several years ago I turned seventy, which is as much as any of us was ever promised. "The days of our years are threescore years and ten" is the King James version of the verse in Psalms that continues, "and if by reason of strength they be fourscore years, yet is their strength labor and sorrow, for it is soon cut off and we fly away."

That strikes me as about right. For most of us, the years up to seventy, give or take a few, are ones we retain our strength in. We're not the same at sixty as we were at fifty, but with a bit of luck, our decline isn't painfully obvious. It only becomes that a decade or so later. By then, we're all on death row.

And so when I was asked by the editor of the Library of Jewish Ideas to choose a topic from a list that was sent me—Judaism and This, Judaism and That—the one that caught my fancy was Judaism and Death. Death had been on my mind for a long time. If I didn't write about it now, when would I?

It occurred to me that I had never thought much about death and Judaism together, not even when, as a boy, I was most scared of the one and most observant of the other. Like all religions, Judaism has developed a complex system of customs, rituals, and beliefs to make death more bearable and understandable. But the thought of his own death to a young boy is *un*bearable, and nothing Judaism might have told me—how I might be mourned, or whether anything would be left of me, or what might be its fate if it were—could have consoled me in the least. Death was a door slamming on a life I wouldn't have; how could Judaism have anything to say about an unlived life? Nor would it have helped to know that it could and that the two contending schools of early rabbinic Judaism, the House of Shammai and the House of Hillel, had disagreed, the first saying it was better not to be born than to be born, the second saying the opposite.

Today, I'm still not ready for death, but I would not feel cheated if it came. It's behaved with more than reasonable restraint. If I haven't used the years as well as I might have despite all the promises made by the boy who begged to live that he wouldn't waste a second of any reprieve given him, that's a common failing. *Eyn adam yotsey min ha-olam v'hatsi ta'avato b'yado* the rabbis said: no one leaves this world with even half his desires fulfilled. We never reach the fifty-percent mark.

When I fear dying now, I fear losing a life that *has* been lived. I fear dying with the knowledge that I failed to accomplish or experience all I was capable of or meant to. I fear an end to the habits and joys I've grown used to. "Truly, the light is sweet and a pleasant thing it is for the eyes to behold the sun," says Ecclesiastes, a book more obsessed by death than any other in the Bible. Truly, it is.

I fear the grief my death will cause others. I fear being parted from those I've loved with a love no boy can imagine. I fear dying without knowing exactly what it was that I lived for.

I muse about the possibility of an afterlife. The idea is infantile, I know: *now I see you again!* But how can a life that has existed cease to exist without a trace? How can the universe have no memory of it?

I chose to write this book because it gave me an opportunity to explore what Jews have thought about such things. I didn't start from scratch. I knew my way around Jewish texts, and you can't have lived in Israel for over forty years as I have without often encountering death in its Jewish forms: Jewish jokes. Jewish prayers. Jewish funerals, Jewish mourning, Jewish memorial rites. One doesn't have to be (and I'm not) a religiously observant Jew to be familiar with them.

There is a vast body of Jewish writing about death. Much of it is halakhic—based in rabbinic law instructing Jews how to behave when someone in their family or community dies. Some is philosophical and homiletic: it advises us how to think about death and how to cope with it intellectually and emotionally. Still another part is visionary, pseudo-visionary, or fabulistic; in it we are told about a next world by authors who either believe they have been given a glimpse of it, pretend to have been given a glimpse of it, or report what has been allegedly glimpsed by others. And finally, there is a growing amount of contemporary literature dealing with all three of these categories, some of it scholarly and some of it consisting of personal reflections.

I've read only a very small amount of all this. As might be expected of beliefs spanning thousands of years and influenced by many different cultures, Jewish attitudes toward death have varied greatly over time. Customs relating to death have changed and changed again. Conceptions of what, if anything, awaits us after we die have evolved and contradicted one another. Jews writing about death have criticized other Jews for what they have held or not held to be true about it. Jews have died with different fears, hopes, and expectations, have been buried and mourned in different ways, and have been considered to survive or not to survive in different forms, all in keeping with the traditions of their time and place.

I've tried to review the most prominent of these traditions and some of the major texts that convey them and to think of my own death in terms of them. In doing so, I've written as the person I am: a man of a certain age and background with certain opinions and biases who lives in a certain place. To write as someone else would have been pointless. Still, perhaps you'll find yourself in these pages, too. After all, we're in this together.

CHAPTER ONE

HAD I BEEN AN ANCIENT GREEK, EGYPTIAN, OR BABYLONIAN living about 1000 BCE, which would have placed me at the start of the Iron Age, the country of death would have been a real place. I would have known how to get there and what to expect on arrival, and the success of my journey would have depended on following the instructions given me.

The map, to be sure, was a crude one. "When in your ship you have crossed the stream of Oceanus, where there is a level shore and the groves of Persephone—tall poplars and willows that shed their fruit—there beach your ship by the deep eddying Oceanus," Circe tells Odysseus in *The Odyssey*, bidding him to visit the dead and consult the shade of the seer Tiresias. "Go yourself to the dark house of Hades; there into Acheron flow Puriphlegethon and Cocytus, which is a branch of the water of the Styx; and there is a rock and the meeting place of the two roaring rivers."

These are rather imprecise directions. Often identified with the Atlantic, which their mariners did not venture out on, the "deep eddying Oceanus" was thought by the Greeks to be a body of water encircling the inhabited earth. Possibly, Odysseus was tasked by Circe with reaching the

Rock of Gibraltar at the western end of the Mediterranean and crossing its straits to their Atlantic side.

Hades, or Erebus, was the Greeks' name for the dead's abode and was alternately situated by them at the ends of the earth, beneath its surface, or both. The Babylonians called this realm Arallu or Ursetu Lo Tari, "the land of no return," and pictured it as a netherworld traveled to along the rivers of the upper earth and through the *abzu,* the primeval depths. For the Egyptians, it was Sekhet-Hetepet, "the fields of peace." Sometimes placed underground by them, too, or by a "lake of flowers" beyond the Nile, it was most commonly located in the heavens. The dead reached it in the boat of the sun god Ra, navigating past Apep, the great dragon of the sky, and the sun's bright circle of flame.

Despite the country of death's different locations, there was agreement that the spirit or soul animating the human body had to have somewhere to go when the body died and did not simply dissolve into nothing. Until challenged by a few of the early Greek philosophers halfway through the first millennium BCE, this belief appears to have been universal; no ancient culture known to us, and no "primitive tribe" studied by anthropologists in our own times, has failed to evidence some form of it. Perhaps human beings were first convinced of the incorporeal existence of a soul by their dream lives at night. In dreams, we go places, see things, and have strange experiences while physically remaining where we are; to the mind of prescientific man, only a part of ourselves that was free to leave our sleeping bodies and return to them could account for this. Death differed from sleep in there no longer being a body to return to. The soul or spirit had to find another home.

Greeks, Babylonians, and Egyptians shared the belief that this new home was reached by boat and guarded by supernatural forces, figures, and monsters, such as the Greek ferryman Charon and his three-headed dog Cerberus; the Babylonian "waters of death" with their fearsome snakes, navigable only by a sailor who delivered his passengers to the seven gatekeepers of the underworld; or the Egyptian *Book of the Dead*'s four man-eating crocodiles of East, West, North, and South. All held that there were appropriate actions and verbal formulas that could appease these beings and permit the dead to proceed on their way unharmed. All imagined that the country of death was reigned over by a deity with an entourage: the toponymic Greek Hades (better known by his Roman name of Pluto), the Mesopotamian queen-goddess Ereshkigal, the Egyptian god Osiris. All thought this country the occasional scene of divine dramas, like that of the Greek myth of Pluto's abduction of the goddess Persephone or the Babylonian story of the descent to Arallu of the goddess Ishtar to rescue her fatally stricken lover Dumuzi.

If you weren't a god, Hades and Arallu could be grim places. The former was populated by shades of the no longer living that flitted endlessly about while experiencing only their own tedium. In the latter, the dead endured a bare existence unless their families managed to intercede with the deities to improve their lot by means of the proper rituals and sacrifices. Otherwise, in the words of the Sumerian-Babylonian epic of Gilgamesh, the king who journeys to the underworld to find his dead friend Enkidu, "dirt is their drink; their food is of clay; like a bird, they wear garments of feathers; light cannot be seen; they dwell in the dark."

The Egyptian heaven was more pleasant but had stricter admission requirements. These called for passing through a hall of judgment in which one's heart was weighed on a scale of truth and justice by a divine court headed by Osiris. If condemned, your soul was devoured on the spot by an "eater of the dead" and annihilated; if judged meritorious, it proceeded to the fields of peace. There, given a new body, you lived a life much like your former one but attended only by enjoyments. The Greeks had their own version of this paradisical afterlife; called Elysium, it was an attractive alternative to Hades that was never integrated with it in their myths. Probably borrowed conceptually from the Egyptians, the Elysian fields, too, were located on the marge of Oceanus. There, according to the poet Pindar, "the good receive a life free from toil . . . . Sea breezes blow around the island of the blessed, and flowers of gold are blazing, some from splendid trees on land, while water nurtures others."

Though a new land to the traveler, the country of death was thus not terra incognita. Yet had I, surrounded by these great cultures of antiquity, been a Hebrew of the same period, which was that of the Judges, the early years of the Israelite monarchy, and the First Temple, I would have been—at least to judge from the Bible—less knowledgeable. Although I would have been prepared when I died for a descent to an underworld like a Babylonian, or like my Canaanite neighbors whose ruler of this domain, the god Mot, had a name like my own word for death, *mavet*, I would have had no notion of how to reach it, of what awaited me there, or if anything much awaited me at all.

This destination was called She'ol, a word of obscure origin with no known cognates in Hebrew or other Semitic languages. While it occurs sixty-six times in the Bible, all but a few of its appearances are passing ones that tell us little. When the Psalmist asks rhetorically, "What man can live and never see death, who can deliver his soul from the power of She'ol?" or God questions Hosea, "Shall I ransom them from the power of She'ol? Shall I redeem them from death?," She'ol is little more than death's poetic synonym.

Yet it is clear from other biblical passages that She'ol was believed to be an actual realm beneath the ground. Thirteen times it is mentioned in conjunction with some form of the verbal root *y-r-d,* "to descend," as when Jacob says of his son Joseph, mistakenly thought by him to have been killed, "I shall go down [*eyred*] in mourning to She'ol, to my son." More graphically, the book of Numbers relates the fate of the rebellious Korah and his camp, "whom, opening its mouth, the earth swallowed . . . and they and all their possessions went down to She'ol." And Ezekiel, prophesying the downfall of the Egyptian Pharaoh and likening him to a mighty tree that will be toppled, declares in God's name: "I will make the nations quake at the sound of his fall and bring him down to She'ol with all who descend to the pit. . . . You [Pharaoh] shall be brought down with the trees of Eden to the land of the below." "The pit" (*bor*) and "land of the below" (*eretz tahtit* or *tahtiyot*) are epithets for She'ol elsewhere in the Bible, too.

About what took place in this realm, the Bible is silent. There are hints that its only activity was a perpetual sleep from which one might be fitfully awakened. Isaiah imagines the *refa'im,* the shades of She'ol, roused from their slumber by the arrival of the slain king of Babylon; like them, he admonishes the newcomer, he will now lie down with "the maggot as your bed and the worm as your blanket." A Hebrew verb used in this prophecy to describe She'ol's stirring is *ragaz,* which has the sense of being troubled or agitated; the dead, it implies, are not pleased to have their sleep interrupted. The word has the same root found in Job's lament, "Why did I not die at birth, come forth from the womb and expire? . . . Then I should have lain down and been quiet; I should have slept and been at rest. . . . There [in She'ol] the wicked have no agitation [*rogez*] and the weary are at rest."

The root *r-g-z* appears again in the most dramatic of all biblical passages about the underworld. This is the story in the book of Samuel about the witch of En-Dor, who is visited by a disguised King Saul seeking to raise the spirit of the prophet Samuel from the dead. Saul is in a precarious mental state. On the eve of a crucial battle with the Philistines, he is exhausted by his futile efforts to apprehend the rebel David and gripped by a sense of foreboding. Having first been crowned by Samuel and then denounced by him and told he will be stripped of his kingship, he badly wants the prophet's pardon and guidance. Hearing of an old necromancer in the village of En-Dor, he rides to her in the dead of night.

The old woman is reluctant to grant Saul's request. During his reign, Saul has sought to stamp out her profession in compliance with the injunction in Leviticus, "Do not turn to conjurers or wizards or be defiled by them," and she, as one of its few remaining practitioners, is apprehensive. Yet reassured that no harm will befall her, she sets to work, and soon the figure of Samuel appears before her, "rising from the earth." Saul, to whom Samuel is invisible, asks her what she sees, and after berating him for concealing his identity, which she has somehow managed to guess, she tells him: "An old man wrapped in a cloak." Convinced the apparition is indeed Samuel, Saul prostrates himself in fear and respect. Samuel, though, is not appeased. "Why have you troubled me [*hirgaztani*] by raising me?" he asks angrily. Saul explains, and Samuel answers sharply, reiterating his prophecy of Saul's doom—which, he predicts, will befall him on the battlefield the next day, when he will join him, Samuel, in She'ol. Samuel then vanishes and the terrified Saul rides off to meet his doom on Mount Gilboa.

It is a mysterious story. What makes the old woman realize her midnight visitor is Saul? Why is Saul so certain, even before the apparition speaks, that it is Samuel? The Bible doesn't say. Yet neither does it suggest that Samuel is a figment of the old woman's or Saul's imagination. He has been raised from the dead and is annoyed.

Presumably, Samuel, like Isaiah's *refa'im,* is an incorporeal shade, a ghostly outline of a once living body that will go back to sleep when its brief ascent from She'ol is over. His status as a prophet has earned him no special benefits there, just as the kings of Egypt and Babylon suffer no exceptional torments for having been tyrants. She'ol is not a place of reward and punishment; all its inhabitants are treated equally. It is a vast subterranean space in which the spirits of kings and paupers, the noble and the villainous, lie side by side.

Had I lived and died then, my spirit would have lain with theirs. How would it have gotten to this place? Who would have guided it? Would it have dreamed of doors opening and shutting, hands thrusting it into darkness, a rough voice bidding it to find a resting place—or would these have been real sounds reaching it in its sleep as more and more dead were crowded into an airless dungeon that, however immense, could barely accommodate their legions? They shuffle into it with heads bent, scraping the low ceiling, stumbling on bodies in the dark, groping the damp earth for a space to lie down in. There are curses, the groans of troubled sleepers, the rasp of a snore. Who would want to awake to any of this? Sprawled around me are the forms of men, women, and children, none of whom I know. It would be impossible to find a familiar face in this perpetual night, let alone a face once loved in the sunlight. And if I found one, what pleasure could it give either of us? Any memories we might share would be intolerably painful. We could only lament our fates and crawl back to our places before they were snatched by new arrivals. Better to sleep—to stay asleep—to fight off all disturbance of sleep.

Such a scene, of course, has no biblical basis. The Bible's reticence about She'ol, when contrasted with the elaborate descriptions of the afterlife in the mythologies of other ancient peoples, is consistent with the biblical demythologization of the world in general, whether in respect of its creation, its governance, or its unseen dimensions. In a universe made and ruled by a single, unrivaled God, there is no room for an independent kingdom of death with a divine cast of actors and a multitude of human extras. Conceivably, one could imagine such a realm ruled by the dead themselves under God's tutelage. Yet this would have called for God's involvement in their affairs—and the God of the Bible, though life and death are in His hands, is a God of the living, not of the dead. Death is not an integral part of His creation. Had Adam and Eve not disobeyed him in the Garden of Eden, the biblical *gan-eden*, the punishment of death would have been unnecessary. It is a catastrophe that should have been averted.

The Bible stresses this. "See, I have set before you this day life and good, death and evil," God has Moses tell Israel in the book of Deuteronomy—and one reason death is evil is that God does not consort with it. He and the dead have no contact. As the Psalmist puts it: "In death there is no remembrance of thee, in She'ol who can give thee thanks?" Isaiah, mocking the conjurers who "chirp and mutter" in their shamanistic rites, attacks the idea that there is anything to be gained from communication with the dead. Though other peoples pray and sacrifice to them, he declares, God's Law teaches that this is fruitless, the illicit crossing of a forbidden frontier. The country of death is in a state of permanent quarantine.

Had I been a biblical Hebrew, indeed, I would have been quarantined from the moment I died. "He who touches the dead body of any person shall be unclean seven days," Mosaic law enjoins. Even contact with a tent or dwelling in which a death has recently occurred demands ritual purification, performed by washing with water mixed with the ashes of an unblemished red heifer ritually slaughtered by a priest. Whoever neglects to do this "defiles the tabernacle of the Lord" and is "cut off from Israel"—a punishment whose very vagueness evokes dread.

Not that my dead body would have been left unattended. On the contrary: burying it, despite the pollution this entailed, would have been a stern duty. Few fates were more feared than the abandonment of one's corpse to the elements or to eaters of carrion. "And your carcass shall be food for the birds of the sky and the beasts of the earth," threatens Deuteronomy in its dire catalogue of the evils in store for the people that strays from God's path. This was something to be avoided at all costs.

More than one biblical narrative deals with such situations. In the book of Kings, we are told of a "man of God" from the southern kingdom of Judah who is sent on a divine mission to rebuke the sinful ruler of the northern kingdom of Israel, Solomon's son Jeroboam. Enjoined neither to eat nor to drink in the place of the encounter, the Judean fearlessly executes his assignment and refuses the chastened Jeroboam's offer of refreshment; yet immediately afterward he is approached by a local "prophet" and, hungry from his long fast, is enticed to break bread with him. No sooner has he done so than God tells him in the prophet's presence that, in punishment, "your carcass shall not rest in your forefathers' grave"—and upon leaving the prophet's home, he is attacked and killed by a lion. The prophet, hearing of this, hurries to the site and finds the lion standing guard over the unmolested corpse. Placing the Judean on his donkey, he returns him for burial to his native territory. Moreover, he tells his sons, when he himself dies he wishes to be buried with him. "Let my bones," he says, "lie next to his."

What are we to make of this curious tale? Impelled by admiration for the Judean's courage and guilt for having been his undoing, the nameless prophet is determined to give him a proper burial in his own village, even though this means flouting God's will more brazenly than did the dead man, whose sin, after all, was no more than a momentary weakness of the flesh. And yet not only does God refrain this time from retaliating, but the lion, too, refuses to harm or let harm befall the dead body. Though God's agent, the lion has a will and principles of its own—which include protecting, against God's ostensible wishes, the man it has killed at His behest. Or do both lion and prophet carry out these wishes, God having repented of meting out too cruel a sentence?

Either way, the story affirms what might paradoxically be called the sanctity of the contaminating corpse. Other biblical tales do the same, such as one about Saul's concubine Ritzpa bat Aya—who, after Saul's death, keeps a vigil for months by the unburied bodies of his and her sons, murdered with the complicity of David, the new king. Impressed by her devotion, David orders their remains, together with the exhumed bones of Saul and his son Jonathan, to be buried in the ancestral tomb of Saul's family. (Previously, in a similar act of piety, Saul and Jonathan's beheaded bodies, publicly displayed by the victorious Philistines, have been rescued and temporarily interred by Israelites from Gilead.) Only then, as though appeased, does a famine raging in the land come to an end.

This is not a uniquely biblical theme. One finds it in other cultures, too. The heroine of Sophocles' tragedy *Antigone*, for example, risks her life to bury her dead brother, whose funeral rites have been denied by the despot Creon. But Antigone is concerned mainly with preventing the desecration of her brother's body. For the biblical Hebrew, the significance of burial with one's ancestors—the Bible calls this being "gathered to one's fathers"—was far greater. Even Joseph in Egypt, assured of a grand state funeral for his regally embalmed mummy, asks for it to be transferred one day to the far-off cave of the patriarchs in Hebron, where it can rest alongside the bones of his great-grandfather Abraham, his grandfather Isaac, and his father Jacob. When the Israelites leave Egypt hundreds of years later, they remember to take it with them.

It made sense to treat the bones of the dead with reverence and their flesh with revulsion. The putrefaction of the flesh *is* revolting. It hideously stains the memory of those we have loved. It is the cruelest possible reminder that we are made of corruptible matter. We do not want to see it, touch it, or smell it. We quite literally want to wash our hands of it.

Yet behold a bone. Let it be a plain one—an old one—a bone scoured by time, sun, or earth. Weigh it in your hand. Feel its hardness, its smoothness. Regard its whiteness. Consider its constancy. Stripped of its flesh, it will change no more. It is a suitable symbol of immortality.

Besides seeing to it, then, that my bones were not eaten or gnawed by wild animals, my family and friends would have sought, in biblical times, to bury them with the bones of my ancestors. This was best done in one of the many limestone caves that are common in the hills of Palestine, like that bought by Abraham in Hebron. I once nearly fell into one of these. It was on a near-acre of hillside my wife and I had bought to build our home on in a small farming town near the Mediterranean, soon after moving to Israel in 1970. Exploring an overgrown patch of ground, I lost my footing, plunged several feet through some bushes, and landed in a hidden depression. Facing me was a low entrance cut into rock, topped by a crudely worked lintel. I cleared the dirt blocking it, crawled inside, and found myself in a rectangular chamber some eight feet by twelve. Niches were hewn in the walls, two in the shorter, rear wall and three in each of the side ones. The floor was carpeted with a thick layer of dirt, washed in by centuries of rain.

It took a Talmudist to explain it to me. Opening the tractate of Bava Batra, he pointed to an ancient regulation:

> He who sells a burial place to another, or who comes to possess one, shall make the interior of the cave four cubits by six and shall hollow out eight niches, three on one side, three on the other, and two in the remaining one.

A cubit was about two feet, the distance from my elbow to my fingertips. Soon afterward I returned with some companions, several flashlights, and a shovel. Our excavation unearthed some red pottery and a fragment of a phonograph record bearing the letters UMBA TUMBA on one side and RAEL on the other. "Middle Ben-Gurion dynasty," grumbled the friend who dug it up. It was he who also found the cave's only human remains: the bottom half of a jaw, yellowed like old parchment, with two rear molars intact in their sockets. I brought it to a dentist, who identified it as a middle-aged woman's with gum problems, which had caused irregularities in the alveolar ridge.

She had died, perhaps two-thousand years ago, perhaps a bit more. The heavy stone sealing her family's burial cave, known in Hebrew as the *golel* or "roller," was pushed away; her body, wrapped in shrouds, was laid inside; the roller was rolled back into place. When enough time had gone by for her flesh to decompose (according to later Jewish tradition, this took a year), the cave was reopened and her bones were collected and placed in a niche with those of her ancestors. She had been gathered to them.

Why was half a jaw all we found? Perhaps it had fallen to the ground when the rest of the body was removed to the niche and had been subsequently covered by dirt. In time, the cave was abandoned and the roller rolled away for other use; the contents of the niche were transferred elsewhere or left to be devoured by jackals and hyenas. This explained everything but the phonograph record.

She had been somebody's wife, mother, daughter. For seven days they had publicly mourned her. This was how long Joseph and his brothers grieved demonstratively for Jacob; how long Saul and Jonathan were lamented by the Gileadites; how long Job's comforters sat patiently on the ground beside him before scolding his refusal to be consoled. Job rends his garments, as do other bereaved in the Bible. They dress in rough, itchy burlap, the biblical sackcloth, sprinkle ashes on their heads, and sit in them. The idea was to be not merely uncomfortable, but symbolically abased. Death *was* abasing, a crushing demonstration of human powerlessness.

But it was to be given its due and no more. While countenancing weeping, wailing, and the hiring of professional keeners, the Bible forbids mourners to injure themselves in their zeal to show grief. "You shall not slash your skin nor tear out your hair," Deuteronomy cautions, referring to two customs of bereavement widespread in the ancient Middle East. (Such self-laceration is practiced to this day by some Shi'ite Muslims, who bloody themselves with knives and chains in annually commemorating the martyrdom of their saint, Muhammad's grandson Huseyn ibn Ali.) The prohibition is based, Deuteronomy states, on men and women being "God's children," whose infliction of harm on themselves inflicts it on God as well. Yet it also reflects an aversion to conceding to death too much. Ritual self-wounding in biblical times was a way of sacrificing one's blood to the gods, as can be seen from the story in the book of Kings of Elijah and the priests of Ba'al—who, to induce their god to heed them, slash themselves with swords and daggers until drenched in gore.

Death was a misfortune, not a god to be sacrificed to. When David's infant son, the offspring of his adulterous union with Bathsheba, dies after a brief illness, his servants fear telling him. He has acted like a mourner while the child languished, sleeping on the ground, not eating, washing, or changing his clothes—what might he do now? But when given the news, he rises, washes, dons fresh clothing, goes to pray, and sits down to eat. "While the child was alive," he explains, "I fasted and wept, for I thought: Who knows? Perhaps God will have mercy on me and the child will live. Now that he is dead, why fast? Can I bring him back? I will seek after him but he will not return to me."

When, long afterward, David himself dies, the Bible tells us that he "lay down with his fathers." Like being "gathered" to them, this is a peaceful, soothing expression. Had I lived in David's time, I would have found a different solace for death from that found by Jews in later ages. The survival of a nonphysical part of myself would not have cheered me; nowhere in the Bible is there a positive word about the descent to She'ol. The survival of a physical part, however, would have been a comfort. I would not often, it is true, have had living visitors in my cave. The only sounds there, had I had ears to hear them, would have been the slow drip of rainwater, the dry creep of beetles, the scuttle and scratch of underground vermin. But I would not have been alone. My bones beside my ancestors', my children's bones beside mine, I would have formed part of a never-ending chain.

I could have thought of it this way because I would have
lived in a different world from our own. It would have been
a compact one of small towns and villages in which everyone was acquainted and ties of birth, marriage, and kin-
ship left no one out. The people surrounding me would
have felt the same responsibility for me that I felt for them:
the parents who raised me, the brothers and sisters I grew
up with, the aunts and uncles who never were far, the cousins I played with as a child, the wife with whom I brought
up my children, the neighbors whose door was open to me
as mine was open to them. I would have experienced great
social solidarity and cohesion—and all the rivalries, jeal-
ousies, and restrictions on personal freedom that go with
them. As developed as I may have been as an individual,
my family, clan, tribe, and people would have been exten-
sions of my own self. I could not have conceived of that self
apart from them.

This is why, in addressing its Israelite audience, the
Bible sometimes alternates, seemingly arbitrarily, between
singular and plural language. Here is an example from
Deuteronomy:

All the commandments that I command you [singular]
this day be you [plural] careful to perform, so that you
[plural] may live and you [plural] may multiply and you
[plural] may enter and inherit the land that God promised your [plural] fathers. And you [singular] shall remember the long way on which the Lord your [singular]
God led you [singular] for forty years in the desert. . . .
But if you [singular] forget the Lord your [singular]
God and you [singular] stray after other gods and you
[plural] worship other gods and you [plural] bow down

before them, you [plural] are my witnesses today that you [plural] shall surely perish.

The arbitrariness, however, is not total. In speaking of obeying or flouting God and His commandments, Deuteronomy prefers the singular "you"; in describing the consequences, it favors the plural. What I do or don't do will be rewarded or punished in the aggregate. Although I myself may never reap its benefits or pay its price, my descendants—the Bible calls them my "seed" or "loin's issue"—will. They will dwell in the house I built, plow the field I cleared, get along with the children of the neighbors I got along with, feud with those of the ones with whom I quarreled, live the loves and hates I passed on to them from whoever passed them on to me. Though not yet born, they are already as much a part of me as I will be of them.

Hence, the centrality in the Bible of the motif of childlessness and childbearing. Abraham and Sarah, Isaac and Rebecca, Jacob and Rachel, the parents of Samuel, the parents of Samson: in each case a barren woman miraculously conceives and gives birth to an Israelite hero. Being childless is not just a matter of thwarted parental instincts or of the drearily empty house that a married couple must awake to each day. It is breaking the chain, losing one's only prospect for immortality. This is most probably the meaning of the "cut-offness" that the Bible never defines, though Psalm 109 comes close to doing so when it declares of the sinner and his children: "Let his posterity be cut off; in the next generation, let his name be erased." "That his name be not erased from Israel" is the reason given for the biblical commandment that, should a man die without children, his brother must marry his widow in the hope of having offspring with her. My brother has my blood and my patrimony. The children born to him from my wife will be mine.

"You [plural] are all standing today before the Lord your [plural] God," Deuteronomy continues, "so that He may make of you [singular] His people and He may be your [singular] God, as He has promised you [singular] and as He swore to your [singular] forefathers, Abraham, Isaac, and Jacob. Nor with you [plural] alone do I make this covenant . . . but with him who is standing with us here today and with him who is not yet with us today."

You (singular) are your people (plural)! As long as it exists, so do you.

Would this have calmed death's terrors in me? Not likely. The Bible is full of the fear of death. Precisely because it is, though, there is something bravely unflinching in its view. It looks at death with clear eyes. There are no other-worldly compensations. Life on this earth is all of value that there is. I may not live it for long, but those who come after me will inherit who I was along with what I possessed. That is my only consolation.

Ultimately, it wasn't enough. As First Temple times yielded to those of the Second, and what we call "Israelite" evolved into what we call "Jewish," the world of the Bible's early books changed into that of its late ones. The First Temple's destruction by the Babylonians in 586 BCE, and the mass exile and loss of national independence that followed, put an end to the old sense of life as a slow, organic passage in which each generation bequeathed itself to the next. History now seemed less a smooth flow of time than a discontinuity of ruptures and breaks.

The prophets of the First Temple period had sensed disaster coming and warned of it. Those of the following period had seen it come. They trusted in a radical intervention on God's part to make things whole again, and they imagined this happening not in but out of the natural flow of time, with evil vanishing in a twinkling from a divinely refashioned world. "For behold, I will create new heavens and a new earth, and the former shall not be remembered," promises Second Isaiah in God's name. And Malachi proclaims: "For behold, the day is coming that shall burn as an oven; and all the proud, yea, all the wicked, shall be stubble; the day that comes shall burn them up. . . . Behold I will send you Elijah the prophet before the coming of the great and dreadful day of the Lord."

Elijah, having departed this life according to the book of Kings by ascending heavenward in a chariot, was not, for Malachi, dead. This is the first time in Judaism that we encounter a specific herald, a figure that was eventually to evolve into that of the messiah, associated with a redeemed world to come.

Jews were different from Israelites. They were more varied, more dispersed, more urbanized. They didn't live only in the Land of Israel. Large communities of them now existed in Babylonia, in Egypt, in North Africa, along the Mediterranean coasts of Syria and Turkey, even in Italy. Hundreds of thousands resided in Alexandria; tens of thousands in Rome; an estimated 120,000 in Jerusalem. Few spoke Hebrew any longer; their main languages were Aramaic and Greek. Different schools and interpretations of Judaism developed, some deeply influenced by non-Jewish thought. Many Jews drifted away from Judaism entirely. And at the same time, large numbers of Gentiles entered the Jewish fold. The old homogeneous, cohesive Israelite society was a thing of the past.

No longer was the idea of me and my ancestors living on through my descendants persuasive. Who knew who these descendants might be? My children and grandchildren might end up far away from me. I myself might die far from the place of my birth, too far to be gathered to my fathers. I could no longer assume that my neighbors knew and cared about who I was, or that I and they had anything in common. I could not assume that I would have anything in common with my own progeny. The field I cleared might not be farmed by them. The house I built might be lived in by others. My life was now uniquely my own.

I would have had to think of death differently. What kept it from being the effective end of me? How were the good and bad I had done recompensed—and if they weren't, why trouble to be good? Moreover, if the evil that befell me was not brought about by the actions of my ancestors, what had I done to deserve it? How could a just God inflict on me poverty, illness, bereavement, or premature death without reason or restitution?

Such questions already concerned Jeremiah, who lived to see the First Temple razed. Alluding to a verse in Exodus in which God threatens, at Mount Sinai, to "visit the iniquities of the fathers upon the children," he proclaims that in the future, "no one shall say any more, 'The fathers have eaten a sour grape and the children's teeth are set on edge.' But everyone shall die for his own iniquity; every man that eats the sour grape, his teeth shall be set on edge." Ezekiel, Jeremiah's younger contemporary and himself an exile in Babylon, agreed. "The son," he proclaimed, "shall not bear the iniquity of the father, neither shall the father bear the iniquity of the son. . . . The soul that sins, it shall die." From now on there would be a new kind of divine justice. My deeds would be requited, not in their effect on my offspring or community, but in the course of my own life.

This was a bold departure from the old view. Yet some of the exiles returned from Babylonia; another temple was built in Jerusalem; and life went on as before. Scoundrels continued to prosper and decent men languished as always. The result was a crisis of religious thought. One encounters it especially in two of the Bible's late, Second Temple–period books, Job and Ecclesiastes (or, to call it by its Hebrew name, Kohelet).

The book of Job begins with Job's unwillingness to question God's justice after all ten of his children have been killed by a freak storm while banqueting and carousing. "The Lord giveth and the Lord taketh," is his response, "blessed be the name of the Lord." Only when he himself is stricken by a tormenting disease does he rebel, curse the day he was born, and complain to God, "You know I am not guilty, yet there is none to deliver me from Your hand." For all his anguish over the loss of his children, Job reasons by Jeremiah's paradigm. If they have been punished, it must be for their own sins, the existence of which he has suspected; this is no reason to physically afflict *him*. Nor would his protest be significantly less if his children were still alive. Nowhere in his long indictment of God does he so much as mention them; the idea of being compensated through his descendants does not speak to him. What he demands is an explanation of why he is being scourged in his own flesh when he is innocent of wrongdoing.

Job, the Bible's only formal dramatic work, is elaborately phrased but straightforward. Kohelet, the Bible's only essay, is linguistically simple but maddeningly circular. Its author, who poses as a jaded Jerusalem king convinced that "all is vanity," says now one thing, now another; reverses his positions and reverses his reversals; goes around and around like the winds of which he says, "they blow to the south and turn to the north, they spin and spin and return to where they started." One minute he is a seize-the-day hedonist, the next a somber moralist, the next an advocate of carpe diem once more; he goes from cynicism to pathos and back again; in dizzying succession he tells us to live wisely, to forget about living wisely because it will do no good, and to live wisely after all because it is better than living foolishly. He is either hopelessly bewildered or brilliantly trying to convey what it is like to live in a bewildering world.

The latter possibility is more commensurate with the incisive bite of Kohelet's prose. Despite its great difference from Job, Kohelet's problem is the same: Jeremiah's promise remains unfulfilled and the traditional consolations for life's shortness and unfairness no longer work. "I saw under the sun the place of judgment, and there was wickedness there," Kohelet laments. "And so I thought, God will judge the righteous and the wicked. . . . Yet men are no different from beasts: one end awaits them all. . . . Who knows if the spirit of a man flies upward while the spirit of a beast goes beneath the earth?"

The author of Kohelet, it would seem, has heard of a new doctrine: upon the death of the body, the human soul ascends on high to stand trial on its own merits rather than descending to an underworld in which all are treated in the same indiscriminate way. However, he is skeptical. What reason is there to think it is true?

Kohelet was probably written in the fourth or third century BCE. By then, the idea of an immortal soul that is rewarded or punished for its deeds was gaining currency in Jewish circles. Long part of the popular religion of Egypt, it had been developed philosophically in Greece by Plato and his disciples, the so-called Neoplatonists, who linked it to a belief in reincarnation. (In his *Republic*, Plato's Socrates has a fanciful description of how the soul, ascending to heaven after leaving the body, journeys to the thrones of the Fates, where it chooses to be reborn on earth in a life that will be either virtuous or vice-ridden in keeping with the wisdom it has or has not acquired in its former existence.) Now, the idea of a heavenly judgment traveled back across the Mediterranean to Palestine, spread by the Hellenization of the region that began with Alexander the Great's late-fourth-century conquests in western Asia. Although not a biblical concept, it could point for corroboration in the Bible not only to Elijah, but also to Enoch, the seventh-generation descendant of Adam said by the book of Genesis to have "walked with God, and he was not, for God took him." Both stories were taken to imply the possibility of human existence elsewhere than on earth, in God's presence.

This was one of two new ways of thinking about death that entered Jewish thought in the Hellenistic era. The other is first clearly encountered in the book of Daniel, written in the mid-second century BCE on the eve of the Maccabees' revolt against the Seleucid kingdom of Syria, which had inherited part of Alexander's empire. Daniel is a new kind of biblical book, an apocalyptic prophesy that seeks to bolster its credibility by pretending to have been written in an earlier age and to have predicted historical events that had in fact taken place by the time of its composition. In describing the climax of history that will follow the overthrow of the Seleucids, it proclaims, "And at that time shall [the archangel] Michael stand up, the great prince which standeth for the children of Thy people . . . and at that time Thy people shall be delivered, every one that shall be found written in the book. And many of them that sleep in the dust of the earth shall awake, some to everlasting life and some to shame and everlasting contempt."

The dead, or at least some of them, will rise bodily! A written record, the earliest appearance of Jewish tradition's "Book of Life," has been kept of their deeds, and they will answer for them, not in heaven, but on earth—where, with the arrival of Malachi's "great and dreadful day of the Lord," they will live happily or wretchedly forever after.

Scholars disagree whether a belief in physical resurrection was indigenous to Judaism. Some, claiming it was, cite the chapter of Ezekiel in which the prophet has a vision of the dry bones of the people of Israel coming to life and hears God declare: "And ye shall know that I am the Lord, when I have opened your graves, O my people, and brought you up out of your grave." Others argue that this is a parable of national revival not meant to be taken literally—and that even if intended to be, Ezekiel borrowed the idea from the Persian religion of Zoroastrianism, with which he might have had contact while in Babylonia.

Be that as it may, by the time Judaism entered the rabbinic age after the Second Temple's destruction in the ruinous revolt against Rome of 66–70 CE, the twin notions of She'ol and being gathered to the fathers had vanished from its scheme of things. Replacing them were a heavenly afterlife, on the one hand, and on the other, an earthly resurrection that would coincide with or follow a grand messianic transformation of reality.

The transition was gradual. Because late biblical books like Daniel and the earliest rabbinic literature are hundreds of years apart, our knowledge of the development of Jewish thought toward the end of the Second Temple period depends on sectarian sources, largely produced in Palestine or alluding to events there, that do not belong to rabbinic tradition, such as the Dead Sea Scrolls, sections of the New Testament, and the various Jewish Pseudepigrapha or "spurious writings" that were rejected for inclusion in the biblical canon.

One of the most influential of these writings was the book of Enoch I, whose original Hebrew or Aramaic text— the work, it would seem, of several authors writing fifty to a hundred years after Daniel—was preserved only in an Ethiopian Christian translation. (Three additional works attributed to the biblical character Enoch date to later periods.) Purporting to be a description of a tour of Creation given the man who "walked with God," Enoch I reveals some of the physical mysteries of the universe: what is above the sky and beneath the earth; where the sun, moon, and stars are when absent from the heavens; the source of the winds and why they bring rain, snow, or clear weather; why the days grow longer in summer and shorter in winter; and so on.

Enoch I also discloses, with equal measures of consistency and contradiction, the fate of human beings after death. It is consistent in asserting that every individual receives his just deserts in an afterlife. It is contradictory in describing how and where this occurs. In one place in the text, the souls of all the dead are said to be conveyed to a traditionally underground She'ol, from which on a future day of judgment presided over by an "Elect One"— also referred to as the *mashiah,* the "Anointed One" or messiah—they will be restored to their bodies and to a life of eternal bliss or misery. In another passage, the dead wait quiescently inside a mountain at the ends of the earth. Elsewhere, She'ol is portrayed not as the Bible's shadowy abode of slumber but as a pit of dark flames into which the souls of sinners are cast when they die, while in yet a different account they are made to suffer in a burning cloud in the sky, from which come "cries, wails, and screams of great pain." Meanwhile, the souls of the righteous await resurrection in the company of angels in a heavenly paradise. When the bodies with which they will be reunited rise from the grave, a new sky will be created above a new earth and "a generation of righteous ones shall arise." The stars will shine seven times brighter than before, justice will reign, and sin "shall disappear from upon the earth."

This is confusing. But it is so because it represents a first attempt to harmonize two quite different conceptions of life after death. While all of Enoch I's contributors agree that the climax of human history will be the day of judgment with its resurrection, the book's earlier parts stress this aspect of the afterlife almost exclusively. In them, as in the Bible, the existence of the disembodied soul in an eventless She'ol is of no interest. Only when rejoined to its body will the soul again have value—and then, too, not in itself but as part of a reconstituted psycho-physical unity. The Bible never preaches, as do various Hellenistic religions, a path of mystic contemplation or ascent in which the soul can and must be liberated from bodily constraints.

It articulates a code of commandments that need a body to perform them.

In principle, then, a belief in resurrection on judgment day should have been enough for late Second Temple Judaism. Yet the longer this day took to materialize, the more fundamentally unfair it seemed that, while awaiting their ultimate fate, the souls of the just and the unjust should share the same twilight state. There arose a need for an interim period in which some of the rewards and punishments of the final judgment were dispensed beforehand, so that the administration of justice was not delayed indefinitely. Hence the presence, in the later parts of Enoch I, of a pleasure-filled heaven and a torment-ridden hell, to one or the other of which the soul proceeds directly after death.

By the time we arrive at a later pseudepigraphic work like *The Life of Adam and Eve*—a small book, probably dating to the first century CE, whose original Hebrew version was lost, too—these inconsistencies have been ironed out. The book begins with the death of Adam after his and Eve's expulsion from Eden. Tearfully grieving for her mate, Eve sees a chariot of angels descend and carry his soul to heaven. There, it is dipped three times in a river of fire to purge it of its sin of disobedience, brought for trial before God, and promised reinstatement at the apex of Creation in a resurrected body at the end of days, at which time Satan—Adam and Eve's tempter who disguised himself as a serpent in the Garden of Eden—will be cast forever with his followers into the same fiery stream. Meanwhile, Eve is informed, Adam's soul will reside in the "third heaven," in a celestial Garden of Eden that is a counterpart of the lost earthly one.

Another pseudepigraphic work from the same period, Enoch II, situates paradise in the identical region. There we read:

> And they [Enoch's guides] brought me up to the third heaven and placed me in the midst of paradise. And that place had an appearance of pleasantness that has never been seen. Every tree was in full flower. Every fruit was ripe, every food was in yield profusely; every fragrance was pleasant. . . . And the tree of life is in that place, under which the Lord takes a rest when the Lord takes a walk in paradise. And that tree is indescribable for the pleasantness of its fragrance. . . . And there are three hundred angels, very bright . . . and with never-ceasing voice and pleasant singing they worship the Lord every day and hour.

First mentioned explicitly in mystical texts of the Talmudic period, the existence of seven heavens, one above the other, was undoubtedly a feature of Jewish cosmology in late Second Temple times, too, as it was of Hellenistic thought in general. (This was probably originally suggested by the seven independently moving heavenly bodies known to the ancients, the sun, moon, and five visible planets, each considered to occupy a sphere of its own.) For the Pharisaic or proto-rabbinic Judaism of the age, the seventh and uppermost of these firmaments was the seat of God's throne; the third, perhaps because belonging to Venus, the brightest of the planets, was a temporary resting place for the souls of the righteous. In an epistle to the Christian community of Corinth written several decades before the destruction of the Temple, the apostle Paul, who was raised as a Pharisee, speaks of having been transported to the "third heaven" or "paradise" in a vision so powerful that "whether it was in the body or out of it, I cannot tell."

Thus, by the end of the Second Temple period, the belief had become widespread among Jews that the afterlife had two stages: a prior one in which the soul was judged and dispatched to a postmortem life of reward or suffering, and a subsequent one in which it was reunited with its earthly body and put on trial with it again. Another pseudepigraphic work known as *The Apocalypse of Abraham*, composed soon after the Temple's destruction, reports that reprobate souls pass the first stage in a raging inferno, where they form "a great crowd in the likeness of men." In the early-tenth-century Slavonic translation in which this book has come down to us, this inferno is called *ognina*, a corruption of Greek *gehenna*, which derives in turn from Hebrew *gey hinnom*—literally, "the ravine of Hinnom." This is a shortening of *gey ben Hinnom*, "the ravine of the son of Hinnom," the name of a dry gulch outside the walls of Jerusalem in which, in First Temple times, children were passed through fire as part of the cult, violently denounced by the prophets, of the Semitic god Molech. Henceforward, *gehinnom* and *gan-eden* were to be the standard Hebrew terms for hell and heaven.

When the body died, the soul went to one or the other. Even less than the prophetic literature they derive from, the Pseudepigrapha have no tolerance for ambiguity. Nowhere do they recognize the mixture of better and worse qualities in a single person that characterizes the great narrative books of the Bible, in which finely shaded figures like Abraham, Sarah, Jacob, Rachel, Leah, Esau, Joseph, Moses, Joshua, Samuel, Saul, and David are depicted as neither too flawed to merit our admiration nor too faultless to escape our censure. There is nothing like this in books like Enoch I, *The Life of Adam and Eve*, or *The Apocalypse of Abraham*, where a stark line divides good from evil. Here, the saint and sinner exist in utter contrast, in the next life as in this one.

Various factors helped shape this polarizing view of humanity, many of them the same as those that had led to the new conceptions of the afterlife in the first place. Among these were the larger, more stratified social structures of the Second Temple period, in which there was a greater tendency to identify with one's own small social or religious community against all others; inner divisions within Judaism that pitted group against group and sect against sect, each convinced it held the key to divine truth; widening social gaps between the rich and poor and the powerful and powerless, with all the social resentments and hatreds that these generated; subjection in Palestine to Seleucid and Roman rule that was more distant, more faceless, more rapacious, and more injurious to Jewish pride than was subjection to autocrats from one's own people; a growing sense of the fundamental injustice of the world; a growing fury at it; an intensifying despair that anything could change for the better until everything changed once and for all; a quickening impatience for this to happen.

Politically, such feelings, having peaked at the time of the Maccabean revolt and then subsided, surged to new heights in the revolutionary ferment of the first century CE that unleashed the great revolt against Rome and its upper-class Jewish collaborators. Religiously, they led to the spread of messianic beliefs that held God's "great and terrible day" to be nigh. In practice, politics and religion were inseparable, many of the revolutionaries being fervent messianists and many of the messianists being convinced that the day of judgment would begin with the overthrow of Roman rule in the Land of Israel.

This mood of apocalyptic expectation permeates the New Testament gospels that tell of the life and death of Jesus, whose crucifixion by the Romans took place several decades before the great revolt broke out. (Although written in the revolt's aftermath, the gospels are steeped in the atmosphere that preceded it.) Again and again, Jesus bids his Jewish followers to be prepared for the "kingdom of heaven" or "kingdom of God" that may arrive at any moment. "Let your loins be girded and your lights burning [all night] like men that wait for their lord," he tells them, "so that when he comes and knocks, they may open to him immediately." Clearly, Jesus is talking about the afterlife's second stage, which is so imminent that both stages will be skipped for many of his listeners; when he promises them, "There be some of you standing here that shall not taste of death till they see the kingdom of God," he is saying that they will see the dead rise in their lifetimes. A last judgment will take place, at which the living will be gathered from "the uttermost parts of the earth" and the souls of the dead from "the uttermost part of heaven."

Since a two-stage afterlife is also basic to rabbinic Judaism, the Pharisees must have subscribed to it, too; where they most differed from the first Christians and from Jewish sectarian groups like the Essenes, who probably

authored all or most of the Dead Sea Scrolls, was in seeking to discourage exaggerated messianic expectations. The
Jewish historian Josephus Flavius, a participant in the great
revolt before he deserted to the Romans and took to con-
demning it, ascribed to the Pharisees the view that "every
soul is immortal, but the souls of the good alone pass into
another body [after death], while the souls of the wicked
suffer eternal punishment"—an odd statement on the face
of it, there being no evidence that there were rabbinic Jews
who believed in reincarnation before the Middle Ages. But
Josephus, who favored the Pharisees because they opposed
violent resistance to Roman rule, wished to present them
in a positive light to the Gentile audience he was writing
for. Hence, he deliberately altered their belief in the soul's
restoration to a resurrected body, which cultivated Greek
readers would have found hard to credit, to the Platonic
doctrine of its rebirth in a new one.

Reincarnation *was* the belief of one atypical ancient
Jewish figure, Philo of Alexandria, who preceded Josephus
by a generation. Having only a superficial knowledge of
Pharisaic tradition, he was neither acknowledged nor remembered by the rabbis, so that his work, written in Greek
like Josephus', survived like the latter's only in non-Jewish
circles. The sole known Jewish thinker until medieval
times to attempt a synthesis of Judaism and Neoplatonism,
Philo held that, though nearly all the souls of the dead returned to earth for another cycle of existence, the greatest
reward was reserved for those who by dint of "the vigorous
study of philosophy" freed themselves of the desire for rebirth and embarked upon "an incorporeal and endless life
in the presence of the uncreated and immortal God." Philo
did not believe in resurrection, and given his Platonic view

of the body as a "prison" or "tomb" from which the soul needed to be liberated, such a doctrine could hardly have appealed to him.

Nor, while believed in by most Jews of the late Second Temple period, was an afterlife of rewards and punishments affirmed by all. A group called the Sadducees, relates Josephus, denied its existence entirely. Josephus has little else to say about this group, and brief mentions of it in the New Testament and rabbinic writings do not add greatly to his account. Apparently, it was a social and religious party, led by the Temple priesthood and old Jerusalem aristocracy, that adhered to a strict construction of the Bible and opposed both the free scriptural interpretation of the Pharisees and the messianism of the sectarians. The New Testament gospel of Mark recounts that several Sadducees once asked Jesus what would happen in the resurrection to a woman who, in accordance with Mosaic law, was wed in succession to seven brothers, each having died without fathering children. Which of them, they wanted to know, would be her husband?

This question was a tease, meant to demonstrate resurrection's logical absurdities. But while logic may have been on the Sadducees' side, history was not. They were ancient Judaism's last afterlife skeptics—to which one might add a bit cynically that they could afford to be, belonging as they did to an entitled upper class that was content with its lot and confident of passing it on to its heirs. If a this-worldly recompense for life's hardships was all there was, the Sadducees were the last to have reason to complain—up to, that is, the great revolt and its brutal suppression, after which we hear no more of them. With the Second Temple destroyed and Jerusalem, as Josephus

described it, so demolished to its foundations that nothing was left that could ever persuade visitors that it had
once been a place of habitation, the Sadducees were swept
away, too. With them went the last vestige of the old biblical conception of death.

CHAPTER TWO

THE MISHNAH, REDACTED IN PALESTINE ABOUT THE YEAR 200 CE, is the first canonical text of Judaism to follow the Bible, from whose last books it is separated by time and the traumatic divide of the Temple's destruction. Constituting the first part of the Talmud, it is a legal commentary on the biblical commandments, interspersed with occasional stories about the early rabbis whose learning and opinions it compiles. The Talmud's much lengthier second part, the Gemara, is in turn a commentary on the Mishnah; produced in Babylonia, it was given its final form sometime between 500 and 700. (The "Jerusalem Talmud," a parallel explication of the Mishnah that was the work of rabbis in Palestine, was less important for subsequent generations.) When we speak of Jewish practices and beliefs concerning death in the Talmudic age, therefore, we are referring to a period of approximately half a millennium beginning with the failure of the great revolt against Rome.

Although terse in style, the Mishnah is exhaustively systematic in its treatment of Mosaic law. Each of its six *sedarim* or "orders" is devoted to an overall area, such as tort laws, farming and agricultural regulations, Jewish holiday observance, and so on, and divided into *masekhtot*

or tractates. A small number of "minor" tractates belonging to none of these categories have an independent status
of their own. One, Evel Rabbati, "The Greater Mourning"
(a name distinguishing it from a shorter, mainly lost
work called Evel Zutarti, "The Lesser Mourning"), is better known to Jewish tradition by its euphemistic inver-
sion *Masekhet Semahot*, "The Tractate of Happy Occasions."
Its fourteen chapters list the rabbinic rules pertaining to
death and bereavement as they came to be established in
the early centuries of the Common Era.

These rules divide the events surrounding death into
six phases. The first is dying itself. The second is the in-
terval between death and burial. The third is the burial or
funeral. The fourth is the week that follows it. The fifth is
the remaining weeks up to the passage of a month, and
the sixth, the remaining months up to the passage of a
year. A seventh section of Semahot deals with the trans-
fer or reburial of the deceased's bones at the end of this
year or later.

Although the Bible has no specific commandments concerning mourning, it does mention, as we have seen, various customs connected to it, of which the week-long period
that came to be known in Jewish tradition as the *shiv'a*
or shiva, "the seven [days of mourning]," is one. The tractate of Semahot enumerates this week's practices. During
it, mourners must rend their garments; they must turn
over their beds and sleep on the floor; they must not shave,
cut their hair, trim their nails, wash, wear shoes or fresh
clothes; they must refrain from sexual relations and engage in no commerce. (The biblical sackcloth and ashes
are not mentioned in Semahot and had evidently been discarded by the time it was written.) On the first two days of

the week, mourners are to do no work, stay at home, and answer only "I'm in mourning" when asked how they are. Starting with the third day, they may reply minimally to questions but are still not to initiate conversations. Women may resume their household work and men may labor in their fields and gardens as long as they do so discreetly.

The period of the first month has a biblical basis, too; it may originally have been a span of public grieving reserved for prominent figures, such as Moses—who, we are told in Deuteronomy, was mourned for thirty days. In the *shloshim* or "thirty," Semahot teaches, some of the first week's restrictions are relaxed. Others, such as the ban on cutting hair or changing clothes, remain in force. Gradually, mourners are expected to return to ordinary life. On the first Sabbath after the death, they do not attend synagogue; on the second, they attend but stand in the back; on the third, they take their customary seat but speak to no one; on the fourth, they behave normally; on the fifth, words of condolence cease to be offered them. When the month is over, the only remaining stricture is on taking part in revelry and celebrations. This alone stays in place for the rest of the year unless one is mourning for a father or mother, in which case all the first-month prohibitions are retained until the mourner is "rebuked by his friends" for neglecting his health and appearance. At that point, one may stop.

At least some of Semahot's regulations, however, are based on customs that must have developed in post-biblical times, even if biblical sanction was sought for them. Nowhere in the Bible, for example, is there any mention of a dying person's obligation to confess his sins; yet in decreeing such a duty, Semahot cites as its authority a passage from the book of Joshua that relates how, after the fall of Jericho, an Israelite named Akhan ben Carmi violates Joshua's order to take no plunder from the conquered city and subsequently admits his deed. Before being put to death for it, he is rebuked by Joshua: "Why have you done this harsh thing to us? The Lord will be harsh to you today." On which Semahot comments: "*Today* you are dealt with harshly—but not in the world to come." Although the author of Joshua clearly did not mean to convey that Akhan's confession will be rewarded in an afterlife, the verse was interpreted in such a manner by the rabbis to justify a practice they themselves must have initiated.

Semahot deals with many other things, too, such as who is required to mourn and who isn't (the obligation falls on all next of kin: sons, daughters, brothers, sisters, fathers, mothers, husbands, and wives); the ritual washing and preparation for burial of the dead body; the permissibility of holding funerals for suicides, executed criminals, and victims of violence or accidents whose corpses have been mutilated or are missing; the status of deceased infants; the legitimacy of burial customs not mandated by rabbinic law or borrowed from the Gentile world, such as smashing the deceased's dishes or burying him with his personal items; eulogies; the proper deportment of condolence callers; the case of family members informed of a death days or longer after it has occurred; the sale of burial caves, grave sites, or property containing such sites; and so on. The tractate also discusses potential situations of conflict. What should be done if abstention from work or commerce during mourning's first days results in damage to the mourner's fields, livestock, or business? (Friends and neighbors should undertake the task or transaction in his or her place.) Suppose a family has made advance preparations for a wedding that falls on a day of mourning. (The wedding should be held and the marriage consummated, after which mourning should resume.) These were potential problems that called for practical solutions.

The basic approach of the rabbis in Semahot is to allow sufficient space for grief while channeling it into formulaic expressions and surrounding it with numerous prescriptions that make sure its desirable limits are not exceeded. Death is a blow that must not be faced alone; it requires the support of others; the emotions it arouses must be acknowledged and given voice to; yet they are best expressed in time-tested ways that never carry mourners past the point from which they can find their way back to normal functioning within a reasonable amount of time. Mourning is not just a private affair. It is the concern of the community, which is thrown off balance if one if its members fails to recover from a death quickly enough. Life has its rights, too. If a funeral procession and a wedding procession meet in the streets of a town, Semahot rules, the mourners must turn aside from the path of the bride, since "respect for the living precedes respect for the dead." Should you have to choose between paying a condolence call and attending a celebration for the birth of someone's child, choose the celebration.

Even when life's duties do not take precedence once a death has occurred, they can do so right up to the moment of it. "The study of Torah is not to be interrupted until the dying have died," enjoins Semahot, in illustration of which it tells a story about Rabbi Akiva. When his son Shim'on fell gravely ill, Akiva did not leave the study house [in which he was teaching] but sent messengers to his son's side. The first returned and said, "His condition is critical." Akiva told his students, "Ask [any questions you may have about the lesson]!" The second returned and said, "He's worse." Akiva told them to go on studying. The third returned and said, "He's dying." Akiva said, "Ask!" The fourth returned and said, "It's over." Akiva stood, removed his phylacteries, tore his clothes, and said: "My fellow Jews, hear me! Until now we were obliged to study the Torah. From now on we are obliged to honor the dead."

This story is chilling, but it is not meant as an indictment of Akiva. Rather, it is told in his praise. Precisely because death is so frightful, one must not cede to it an inch more than is necessary. Akiva, from the Mishnah's perspective, was not being heartless. For all one knows, his heart was breaking. He was being self-disciplined, and discipline is never more of a virtue than when maintained in the face of death.

Although the two stories might seem to be opposites—in one, death puts an end to displays of grief, while in the other it permits them to begin—the story of Akiva and his son in Semahot is akin to the story of David and his infant child in the book of Samuel. In both, life comes first. But the early rabbis depart from the Bible with regard to the boundary between life and death. In the Bible, this is not to be crossed. In the Talmud, its porousness is accepted. In the Gemara's tractate of Berakhot, in the midst of a discussion about whether the dead do or don't know what is happening among the living, the argument that they do is made by the following story:

Once there was a pious Jew who, on the eve of Rosh Hashanah, during a time of drought, gave a coin to a poor man and was so roundly scolded for it by his wife that he went to sleep in the graveyard. There he heard two [young women's] ghosts talking. One said to the other, "My dear, why don't we tour the world and listen to what is being said behind the curtain [separating the earthly and heavenly realms] about what new woes are in store." "I can't do that," said her friend, "because I'm buried in a mat of reeds. Why don't you go and tell me what you hear?"

She went and returned. "My dear," asked her friend, "what did you hear behind the curtain?" "I heard," she said, "that whoever sows his wheat in the first quarter [of the growing season] will have it ruined by hail." The Jew went and sowed in the second quarter. Everyone's crop was ruined and his was not.

The next year, hoping to follow up on his success, the pious man again spends a night in the graveyard and again hears the ghosts conversing. This time, too, the woman who is buried in a humble reed mat instead of more expensive cloth shrouds feels she in no state to travel and tells her friend to go to the "curtain" by herself and report back. This the friend does—and now the news is that wheat sown in the second quarter will be ruined by rust. The Jew sows in the first quarter and once more has the only successful crop. Nagged by his wife to explain his good luck, he tells her all. The story continues:

Not long afterward, the man's wife quarreled with the mother of the [dead] young woman and said to her, "Take a look at your daughter [whom you] buried in

49

a reed mat." A year later the man went to sleep in the graveyard again and heard the ghosts talking. "My dear," the first said, "why don't we tour the world and listen to what is being said behind the curtain about what new woes are in store?" "My dear," said the other, "let me be. What should have remained between the two of us is now public knowledge."

The second dead woman is not upset by heaven's secrets having been revealed to the living. What mortifies her is the disclosure of her own secret that she has been shamefully buried in a cheap mat. And the story ends with its anonymous teller declaring triumphantly, "You see, they [the dead] know!"

Similarly, there is no disapproval in this tale of the pious Jew's visits to a graveyard. On the contrary: what he learns there is a reward for his piety. If he has done anything wrong, it is making the mistake of telling his shrewish wife the truth. The biblical wall between the living and the dead has crumbled, partly because, with the loss of the Temple and the purifying ashes of the red heifer dispensed by its priests, the old purity laws have become obsolete. Deprived of the means of removing death's stain, Judaism was forced to overlook it, though a last vestige of it survived in certain restrictions on contact with the dead on the part of *kohanim,* descendants of the priestly caste, to which the tractate of Semahot devotes a chapter.

The old purity laws are also dealt with in the Mishnah, though on a purely theoretical basis. (The rationale for this was the belief that the Temple would be rebuilt one day, so that everything pertaining to it needed to be recorded for future use.) The tractate that does this is called

Ohalot, "Tents," because of the biblical ruling that contact with anything under the roof of a tent or dwelling harboring a corpse renders one impure, and it examines different possible situations. Suppose a house in which someone has died shares a wall with another house: is the latter rendered impure, too? If a part of a house is unroofed, such as an inner courtyard or a hearth with a chimney, is it free of impurity? Can an item removed from an impure dwelling spread its impurity to an item elsewhere—and if so, under what circumstances?

Death's contaminating power is treated by Ohalot as if it were an invisible physical force, able to pass through some things and not others, to spread to certain objects but not to all, sometimes to dissipate and vanish and sometimes to remain potent and toxic. Highly penetrating, it is also highly abstract, stripped of all the physically and spiritually disagreeable features that caused the Bible to cordon death off, and lacking the slightest practical significance for its era. This is what made community graveyards like the one spoken of in Berakhot possible in Judaism, a religion that had in earlier times buried its dead in single-family enclosures. Once contact with the dead was no longer an issue, they could be freely concentrated in a public space.

As a common Jewish burial practice, interment in the earth probably started in Babylonia, whose flat terrain had few or no caves. In Palestine, the shift from the private cave to the communal graveyard passed through the intermediate stage of the catacomb. There is no better place to see this happening than the site of Bet-She'arim, at the eastern foot of Mount Carmel, over whose grassy thirty acres I wandered one balmy winter day with a half-dozen other tourists.

In the late second century CE, the town of Bet-She'arim, whose ancient ruins lie on a hillside overlooking the site, was the seat of the Sanhedrin, the supreme source of rabbinic jurisdiction in the centuries following the destruction of the Temple. Presiding over it was Yehuda ha-Nasi or Judah the Prince, the most powerful rabbinic leader of his and perhaps any age. The scion of a fabled rabbinical family, and a man of wealth, influence, and close ties with the Roman authorities governing Palestine, it was he who oversaw the written redaction of the Mishnah, until then a loose body of oral law. In it he is often referred to simply as "Rabbi," as if no one else deserved the title as much as he did.

It was Judah the Prince's death that turned Bet-She'arim into the major necropolis that it became. Despite his having transferred the Sanhedrin toward the end of his life to the town of Tsippori in the Galilee, Bet-She'arim was where he wished to be buried, and a family cave was prepared for him there. (Jerusalem, where his family had its roots, had been barred to Jews by the Romans and Jewish burial was no longer practiced in it.) He died about the year 220, after a long illness. The many rabbis gathered by his bedside, the Talmud relates, sought to stave off his end by fasting and praying for divine mercy until a household servant, pitying her master's suffering, dashed a clay pot to the ground; startled by the sound of its shattering, the vigil keepers were distracted and Judah the Prince passed away. "The angels above and the titans below battled for the Holy

Ark," his disciple Eleazar Bar-Kappara is said to have exclaimed, "and the angels vanquished the titans."

There had been a scattering of burial caves at Bet-She'arim before that, hewn from the soft limestone of the hillside by local families. Judah the Prince's, though, was far larger and grander. A monumental arch rose eight meters above its entrance, which was framed by stone pilasters bearing a heavy lintel and shut by a ornamentally embossed double door whose massive stone slabs, swinging on slender hinges carved from the bedrock, were opened by a key that raised an inner bolt. Yet the Talmud tells us that Judah requested to be buried in simple shrouds with his body touching the soil of the Land of Israel, and his and his wife's plain stone coffins at the rear of the cave were fashioned, unusually, without bottoms.

In time, others were buried in the same cave. Among them, as attested by the few surviving inscriptions on its walls, were Judah's two sons Shim'on and Gamaliel; his disciple Hanina bar Hama; and Gamaliel's granddaughter Atian, dead at the age of "nine years and sixth months, may her place be with the righteous." Buried beside her was Atio, "the daughter of Rabbi Gamaliel ben Nehemiah, who died unmarried at the age of twenty-two." The two must have been cousins, Atio's father having been named for his grandfather, Yehuda ha-Nasi's son.

The cave was reserved for Yehuda's family and close circle. Yet after he was laid to rest in it, something new began to happen at Bet-She'arim. Hearing of his decision, Jews from elsewhere chose to emulate it. Soon numerous other caves were being hollowed from the hillside, the scalelike strokes of their excavators' chisels visible on the ceilings to this day. Some were small, holding only a few bodies;

others, large enough to accommodate hundreds. These were commonly divided into separate chambers, each sealed by its own heavy door, sometimes having second stories and attic tombs reached by stairs. An even greater space saver was the traditional custom of periodically collecting the dead's bones. Removed from their sarcophagus (the Greek word for a stone coffin literally means "flesh-eater"), which was then reused, they were transferred to an ossuary, a small container placed in a niche or vault in the cave's walls. Hence, all the inscriptions at Bet-She'arim are found on these walls, not on the nameless sarcophagi.

While brief, these inscriptions tell the story of the place. Most are in Greek, then the main language of the eastern Mediterranean world. Others are in Hebrew or Aramaic. Some typical ones read:

"Here lies Shim'on son of Yonatan, and whoever opens [his tomb] will, under pain of oath, come to a bad end."
"Daniel, son of Ado of Tyre."
"Lord, remember your servant Sarkados." Above this, perhaps referring to Sarkados's wife: "Lord, remember your maidservant Primosa."
"This is the grave of Aidyseus, head of the council of elders of Antioch." There follow the names of other members of Aidyseus' family.
"Benjamin the cloth merchant, son of the most excellent Macrobius," and beside it, "Sabiris son of Sabirus, chief cloth dyer."
"The head of the synagogue of Sidon."
"Germanos, son of Isaac the Palmyrian."
"In memory of Calliope, freed bondwoman of Procopius, glory to his memory."

"This is the grave of Rabbi Yitzhak bar Mekim, *shalom*."

"Here lies Theodosia of Tyre, also known as Sarah."

The longest and most literary epitaph, written in Greek hexameter, is:

"Here lie I, dead, son of Leontius, son of Sappho-Iustus. After I plucked the fruit of wisdom I left the light, my woeful parents who mourn ceaselessly, and my brothers. Woe to me in my Besara [Bet-She'arim]! . . . I, Iustus son of Leontius, lie here with many of my people, for so willed stern fate. Be comforted, Iustus: no man is immortal."

Alongside such inscriptions, the sarcophagi and cave walls display a large number of graphic depictions, engraved, drawn, or chiseled in bas-relief. Many are of Jewish symbols, most commonly the menorah or seven-branched candelabrum; also found are the ram's horn, the citron, the palm branch, the Ark of the Tabernacle, and the twin lions of Judah. Other illustrations are informative, symbolic, or merely decorative. Next to the epitaph of Germanos is the figure of a gladiator, perhaps because he was one. (Jewish gladiators were not unknown in Roman times—the renowned third-century rabbi Shim'on ben Lakish earned a living as one as a young man.) Pictures of ships, birds, winged seraphs, and the like, all representing the journey to another world, abound, too, along with geometrical patterns. Most are crudely executed. There are, however, exceptions, such as a sarcophagus with an artfully rendered illustration of the Greek myth of Leda and the swan found near the epitaph of Iustus.

What can be deduced from all this?

First, that the catacombs of Bet-She'arim served a far-flung population. Places named in the inscriptions like Antioch, in the north of Syria, or Palmyra, in its eastern desert, were hundreds of miles away.

Second, that much of this population, while undoubtedly Jewish, was highly Hellenized and did not necessarily lead a rabbinically normative life. Many of the dead bear Greek rather than Hebrew names, or a combination of the two.

Third, that most of the caves were not single-family ones. Many of those buried in them do not seem to have been accompanied by kin. Some apparently belonged to other kinds of associations. One large cave appears to have housed only bodies from Syria and was possibly the property of one or more Syrian Jewish fraternal organizations. Part of the catacomb known as "the cloth merchants' cave" may have been owned by a professional guild.

In short, the Bet-She'arim catacombs were, like a modern cemetery, a commercial enterprise selling space. Whether this was administered centrally, or whether residents of the town sold plots of land on their own, any Jew wishing to be buried at the site and able to afford it could do so. This could not have been cheap. The cost of transportation alone—the bones of some of the dead probably arrived in ossuaries, while the bodies of others were shipped intact in wooden caskets—would often have been great. The practice could only have developed in an age in which people were more aware of themselves as individuals, and more conscious of having their own separate fate after death, than in the past. There were now well-off Jews who cared less about resting in the bosoms of their families after they died than about lying in proximity to a celebrated figure like Yehuda ha-Nasi. A grave at Bet-She'arim was prestigious.

It was not only that, though. In Genesis Rabba, a fourth-century compilation of Midrash, the rabbinic corpus of imaginative and homiletic literature, there is a story about Judah the Prince. He and Rabbi Eleazer ben Pedat, it is related, were once walking outside the gates of Tiberias—a city on the Sea of Galilee, on the eastern border of the Land of Israel—when they saw a casket being brought for burial from Syria. "What good does it do to breathe one's last outside the land and be buried in it?" Eleazar remarked angrily. "It makes me think of the verse [in Jeremiah], 'And ye have defiled my land and made my heritage an abomination.' You abominate it [by living elsewhere] in your lifetime and you defile it [with your corpse] in your death."

Judah chided his companion with a biblical verse of his own. "When someone is buried in the Land of Israel," he replied, "God forgives him all his sins, for it says, 'He will make expiation by his land for his people.'" The Hebrew of this verse is obscure and in all likelihood contains a scribal error; it certainly did not originally have the sense that Judah attributed to it. Moreover, the story itself is probably apocryphal, since Eleazar, though he studied in Tiberias in the mid-third century at the academy of Judah's student Yohanan bar Nafha and succeeded him as its headmaster, was born and raised in Babylonia and is unlikely ever to have met Judah. Yet the kernel of truth in it may be that Judah did believe in the expiatory power of burial in the Holy Land—and even if he didn't, it was the spread of such a belief in his age that helped make Bet-She'arim a sought-after site. Jews from the Diaspora paid to be buried there because they thought it would improve their prospects in the afterlife.

Just how they conceived of this life is far from clear. Classical Midrash, whose period of composition extends to the end of the Talmudic era, is reticent on the subject. Perhaps this reflects the sentiment expressed by Yohanan bar Nafha, who, citing the verse in Isaiah, "Neither has the eye seen . . . what He has prepared for those who wait for Him," took this to be a reference to "the world-to-come." The future wonders spoken of by the prophets, Yohanan held, pertained only to the earthly coming of the messiah, not to any other-worldly reality, about which even a prophet like Isaiah knew nothing.

Not all agreed about the coming of the messiah. Equated by some with the resurrection, it was disassociated from it by others; indeed, there were rabbis like the third-century Babylonian leader Samuel who maintained that the sole difference between the messianic age and our own would be the restoration of Jewish political independence. The very term "the world-to-come," Hebrew *olam ha-ba,* while occurring repeatedly in early rabbinic literature, is frustratingly ambiguous, referring sometimes to the first stage of the afterlife, sometimes to the second, and sometimes to both. In the well-known remark of Judah the Prince's teacher, Ya'akov ben Kurshai, "This world is like a vestibule leading to the world-to-come; prepare yourself in the vestibule so that you may enter the banquet hall," it is hard to say which of these three possibilities applies.

Furthermore, even when the rabbis offer details of the afterlife, these frequently clash with one another, as rabbinic opinions in the Talmud and Midrash tend to do; nor, often, is it ascertainable how literally they were meant to be taken or how much they reflected or shaped the thinking of the average Jew of the times. Take the case of another third-century rabbi, Yehoshua ben Levi. A man to whom legend ascribed a friendship with the prophet Elijah, he is credited by a midrash with persuading the Angel of Death to give him an advance look at paradise before his death. As they were on their way there, the tale goes, he asked to hold the angel's sword, and when lifted for a glimpse over heaven's walls, he leaped to their other side after wriggling loose from the angel's grasp and refused to give the sword back. Had God not demanded its surrender, there would have been an end to death in the world, for the Angel of Death—a creature imagined by the rabbis as "full of eyes"— needed his sword for his work. Brandishing it, another midrash tells us, to frighten his victims, to whom alone he was visible, he dripped a drop of fatal poison from its tip into their mouths as these opened wide with terror.

Yehoshua ben Levi, the same story relates, next refused to return to earth in order to die there, and this time God relented and permitted him to remain in paradise. Another, longer midrash contains a supposed report of what he saw there. Part of it reads:

> There are two gates of chalcedony in the Garden of Eden, and around them, sixty myriads of ministering angels, the radiance of the countenance of each shining like the splendor of the firmament. When a righteous man arrives, they remove from him the garments in which he abode in the grave and clothe him in eight garments of clouds of glory. . . . Then they bring him to a place of water brooks encompassed by eight hundred species of roses and myrtles. Each and every righteous man is

given a canopy in keeping with the honor due him. Out of it flow four rivers, one of milk, one of wine, one of balsam, and one of honey. Each and every canopy has above it a vine of gold in which thirty pearls are set, and the brightness of each shines like the brightness of the planet Venus. Each and every one has under it a table made of precious stones and pearls. Sixty angels stand at the head of each and every righteous man and say to him: "Come and eat honey in gladness, because you have occupied yourself with the Torah, which is likened to honey; and drink wine stored in its grapes since the six days of creation, because the Torah is likened to wine." . . . There is no night there and its usual three watches keep changing. In the first watch, each man becomes a child in the company of children and rejoices as children rejoice. In the second watch, each becomes a youth in the company of youths and rejoices as youths rejoice. In the third watch, each becomes old in the company of old men and rejoices as old men rejoice.

There are also in the Garden of Eden eighty times ten thousand trees in each of its quarters, the smallest of which is more finely scented than the finest spices. In each quarter are sixty times ten thousand angels, singing in sweet voices, and the Tree of Life is in the middle, its branches covering the entire garden. It bears five hundred thousand kinds of fruit, each differing in taste; the appearance of one is not like that of another, nor is the fragrance of one like another's. Clouds of glory hover above it and breezes blow from every direction, wafting the scent from world's end to world's end. Under it sit the disciples of the wise [*talmidey hakhamim,* the Hebrew term for rabbinic scholars], studying the Torah. . . .

[And] among them sits the Holy One Blessed Be He, ex-
pounding it to them.

This midrash is first found in a medieval source and
may contain post-Talmudic elements. Much of it, however,
rests on older traditions going back to the "third heaven"
of Enoch I and Enoch II, some of whose features can also
be found in Talmudic stories, such as one about the poor
scholar Rava bar Avuha. Briefly transported to paradise, he
was given a gift of wonderfully fragrant leaves. Not want-
ing to profit from them upon his return to earth, where
they were worth a fortune, he threw them away; yet the
cloak they were wrapped in remained so redolent of them
that he sold it for a large sum and never had to worry about
money again.

Yehoshua ben Levi's three watches of the night, on the
other hand, are unique. They purport to answer the question, traditionally posed as a logical objection to immortality: which of the many ages that I have been in this world
will I be in the next one? If it is the age I died at, I may be
too old for the pleasures of youth that I long to regain; if
a younger one, I will be deprived of a part of my experience and reduced to a truncated version of myself. The midrash addresses this problem by proposing that I will be all
of my past ages, going from one to another while partak-
ing of the best of each. An ingenious solution, this trans-
lates an inner reality (for are not the child, the boy, and the
younger and older man that I was all still alive in me?) into
an outward one.

But of course, this only creates new difficulties. Suppose
I die at the age of sixty while my children live into their
seventies. If in the third watch of paradise both I and they

are the age we were at our deaths, I will be younger than they are; yet if paradise's inhabitants continue to grow older, some of them will be thousands of years old when I join them. This is but one of the conundrums that arise when human life, which is lived in time, is imagined under the aspect of eternity.

And again: how, without its bodily sense organs, will my soul feel or perceive? Perhaps Yehoshua ben Levi conceived of its having an angelic or "astral" body, a vehicle resembling its earthly one but of a finer substance. Found in Neoplatonism, the notion of an "ethereal matter" in which the disembodied soul is clothed appears in early Christianity, too. Paul, in his epistle to the Corinthians, speaks of "a natural body and a spiritual body," so that "the glory of the celestial body is one thing and the glory of the terrestrial is another." But this, too, only raises more questions. Will my celestial body be a more perfect replica of my terrestrial one, complete with skin and nerves? If not, how will it see, hear, or touch other souls, or enjoy any of heaven's delights? If so, must it not feel pain along with pleasure, since the terrestrial body's capacity for the one is necessarily equal to its capacity for the other?

Our midrash divides the inhabitants of paradise into two classes. For most, it is a place of joyful activity akin to life on earth but free from all worry and unhappiness. For a select few, gathered around the biblical Tree of Life, it is devoted to rabbinic Judaism's highest value of religious study. May everyone join them? Not according to a story in Kohelet Rabba about Shim'on ben Lakish and a potter who brings a jug of water every day to the cave in which Ben-Lakish sits studying Torah. "Rabbi," the potter asks one time, "do you remember how we went to school together as boys? You were fortunate [to become a scholar] and I wasn't. Pray for me that in the world-to-come I will sit by your side [and study with you]." "What prayer can I offer for you?" Ben-Lakish replies. "Don't you know that [in paradise] you will be with your fellow craftsmen? Everyone is placed there according to his profession." A cruel answer— but how, even in paradise, can a potter expect to keep up with rabbis?

More ambiguous is a tale in the Gemara's tractate of Pesahim about Yehoshua ben Levi's son Yosef, who was said to have fallen ill, been given up for dead, and miraculously recovered. "What did you see [in the afterlife]?" he was asked by his father, who had not yet made his own trip there. "I saw an upside-down world," Yosef answered. "Those on top [in this life] were on bottom and those on bottom were on top." "And we?" his father pressed him. "As we are here, so we are there," replied Yosef. Presumably, he meant that while this world's rich and mighty rank behind its poor and downtrodden in the world-to-come, rabbinical scholars, whether rich or poor, are equally esteemed in both.

Is a vision of the afterlife like that attributed to Yehoshua ben Levi a serious one? Or is it merely a promotional tableau, designed to make ordinary Jews desirous of living lives worthy of it? The Babylonian sage Rav, who also studied with Judah the Prince, thought the latter was the case. "The world-to-come," he declared,

is not at all like this world. In the world-to-come, there is no eating, no drinking, no procreation, no commerce, no jealousy, no hatred, no rivalry. The righteous sit with crowns on their heads and enjoy the radiance of God's presence.

Paradise, Rav insists, is not a perfected this-world in which earth's enjoyments are enhanced and its tribulations banished. Its only pleasure is the bliss of bathing in divine light. This is an assertion not previously found in Jewish sources. Taking into account the different modes of expression of rabbinic and Greek thought, it has an affinity with a statement like that of Rav's Neoplatonist contemporary Plotinus, who wrote:

> [A man] will not doubt that he is immortal when he sees himself in the world of pure intelligence. He will see his intelligence occupied, not in the observation of some sense-object that is mortal, but in thinking of the eternal by an equally eternal faculty. He will see all the entities in the intelligible word, and he will see himself become intelligible, radiant, and illuminated by the truth emanating from the Good, which sheds the light of truth on all intelligible entities.

Like Philo, Plotinus held that, freed from the body, the enlightened soul experiences nothing but the joy of pure knowledge, no longer cloudily filtered through its physical organs as knowledge is on earth, but illumined by a direct perception of the Divinity. Indeed, if one substitutes "the light of Torah" for "the light of truth"—and the Torah, to the rabbinic mind, *is* truth—one arrives at a conception not only like Rav's but like Yehoshua ben Levi's exposition of the Law by God in paradise to "the disciples of the wise." Paul was saying something similar when he declared, "For now [in this life] we see through a glass darkly, but then [in the next life] face to face; now I know in part, but then shall I know even as also I am known." To know as one is known is to know as God knows, with an unmediated and comprehensive grasp of all things.

When it comes to conceptions of the afterlife in the early centuries of the Common Era, Judaism, Christianity, and Hellenistic philosophy often shared a single universe of discourse, with Christianity standing midway between the concreteness of the rabbis and the abstraction of the philosophers. Yehoshua ben Levi's description of the righteous studying in heaven has close parallels in the early Christian church fathers. The third-century Origen wrote in his *De Principiis:*

> When we were upon earth, we saw either animals or trees, and beheld the differences among them, and also the very great diversity among men; but although we saw these things, we did not understand the reason of them. . . . I think, therefore, that all the saints who depart from this life will remain . . . in some classroom or school of souls, in which they are to be instructed regarding all the things which they had seen on earth, and are to receive also some information respecting things that are to follow in the future.

Whether most Jews or Christians of the age would have found sitting in a heavenly classroom or sunning themselves in divine splendor sufficiently enticing to motivate their earthly behavior is questionable, which is why an idyllic pleasure park may have been a necessary lure. Yet apart from such an Elysium's logical contradictions, there is a psychological realism to Rav's rejection of it. There are three things, the Gemara's tractate of Hagigah states, that distinguish human beings from the angels:

their "eating and drinking like animals, their excreting like animals, and their procreating like animals"—and a paradise whose inhabitants eat, drink, excrete, and have sex and children cannot possibly be angelic in its perfection. Even allowing for non-inebriating elixirs and inoffensive excrement, the fly in the ointment would still be sex and children.

Indeed, is not the very thought of a child in a perfect world contradictory? The souls admitted to paradise have earned their place there by living virtuously, and it is the virtue they have acquired that enables them, presumably, to coexist in harmony. Yet children are not virtuous and must be educated to become so, slowly and painfully. They cannot be prevented from being selfish or unreasonable, or from quarreling and fighting—and what is more, from being the cause of fights and quarrels, since even in paradise I would feel a greater love for my own child than for the child of someone else. In this life, quarreling children lead to quarreling adults. How could this fail to be true of another life?

And all the more so when sex is involved. Is it at all possible to love sexually without feeling envy of my rivals and sadness, anger, or even hatred when spurned or bested in the competition? This, rather than any revulsion toward sex, is why it must be barred from Rav's paradise. It is why Jesus answers the Sadducees' teasing question about the seven husbands by telling them, "When they [the husbands] rise from the dead, they neither marry nor are given in marriage, but are as the angels which are in heaven." The angels, the ancients agreed, were sexless.

But how can I look forward on earth to being sexless in heaven, or even to a life free of pain, disappointment, and loss? Just as the possibility of pleasure depends on that of pain, so the possibility of achievement depends on that of failure and the possibility of happiness on that of misery. Here lies the paradox of paradise; for either I conceive of it as an ideal version of this world, only to realize that no credible version of this world can be ideal, or I think of it as something else entirely—and why, then, creature of this world that I am, should I strive to gain entry to it? This is the reason that all descriptions of heaven disappoint. They are either jejunely flat like Yehoshua ben Levi's or unsatisfyingly rarified like Rav's.

For this reason, too, every heaven must have its hell: not simply to punish evildoers (who, if heaven were so appealing, would be punished enough by their exclusion from it), or to create a spiritual balance like the symmetries that govern the physical universe, but to encourage conduct insufficiently spurred by the idea of heaven alone. The Mishnaic sage Eleazar ha-Kappar had this in mind when he said:

> Whoever is born is destined to die, and whoever dies is destined to live [again], and whoever lives [again] is destined to be judged. . . . And do not let your worse self reassure you that the earth will be your refuge, for you were conceived without being asked, and you were born without being asked, and you live without being asked, and you will die without being asked, and without being asked you will be held accountable by the King of Kings, the Holy One Blessed Be He.

Faced with a simple choice between heaven and the grave, one might be tempted to choose the laxer life and the grave. A greater deterrent than the grave is called for.

About the actual nature of hell, early rabbinic literature
is as unforthcoming as it is about that of heaven. The
one punishment clearly associated with hell was fire, already its defining feature in the age of the Pharisees and
the Pseudepigrapha. An originally Talmudic-period story
about Rabbi Akiva, found in greater detail in later versions,
relates how, while walking on a lonely road one day, he
encountered a soot-blackened man running with a load of
wood on his back. Asked where he was hurrying, the man
replied that he was a Jew being punished in Gehenna for his
sins, the worst of which was having impregnated another
man's bride, and that he was required to gather and bring
the firewood over which he was roasted each day; if late
in arriving with it, he would be flogged with fiery lashes.
The story ends with Akiva finding the sinner's illegitimate
son, seeing to it that he performs the rite of circumcision
that he never underwent as an infant, and teaching him
the Jewish prayers. (Akiva was an appropriate figure for
this story, since he himself, according to tradition, had no
Jewish education when young.) When the son attends synagogue for the first time and proclaims, "Bless God the
Blessed One forever and ever," which is the congregation's
response to the prayer leader's call to prayer, his father is
released from Gehenna and admitted to paradise.

This tale treats hell as a place on earth—or rather within
it, with an opening to the world above. So, it would appear,
the rabbis of Talmudic times pictured it. In the Gemara's
tractate of Eruvin is the statement that Gehenna has three
hidden entrances, "one in the desert, one in the sea, and one
in Jerusalem," where puffs of smoke rising from the ravine

of Ben-Hinnom mark the underground fires burning there. And in the tractate of Bava Batra, the third-century rabbi Rabba bar bar Hanna tells of being taken by a Bedouin to the place in the desert where the rebellious Korah and his followers were swallowed by the earth for defying Moses. Smoke rose from it, accompanied by the lament, "Moses and his Torah are true and we are liars"; the rebels, the Bedouin said, could be heard confessing their guilt every thirty days, when Gehenna, "turning them like meat in a stew pot, returns them to this spot." Although Rabba bar bar Hanna was known for his tall tales, the tallest tale still reflects the assumptions of the society it is told in—one supported in this case by the knowledge that the earth has underground sources of heat manifested in volcanoes, hot springs, and geysers.

Traceable to the biblical She'ol and the underworld of pagan antiquity, hell's subterranean location is also part of early Christian tradition. In its concern for the suffering of hell's inmates and the shortening of their stay there, however, the story of Rabbi Akiva is distinctly Jewish. Christianity, starting with the New Testament, insisted on "the doom of fire without end and without break," as the church father Tertullian put it, with no possibility of remission or pardon. For the early rabbis, on the other hand, the punishments of Gehenna were, at least for some, commutable. Akiva is credited by the Mishnah with the belief that the sinful are sentenced to hell for a maximum of twelve months. Shim'on ben Lakish, punning on the verse in the Songs of Songs, *k'felah ha-rimmon rakatekh*, "Your brow is like the curve of a pomegranate," reads *rakatekh*, "your brow," as *reykatekh*, "your worthless one"; since by virtue of participating even minimally in Jewish life, he declares,

the most worthless sinner performs as many commandments as a pomegranate has seeds, the fires of hell have
"no power" over him. By this Ben-Lakish may have meant
not that such a person escaped hellfire entirely, but that its
pain was bearable for the limited time it had to be endured.

The most extensive treatment of hell in early rabbinic literature is in the tractate of Rosh Hashanah—a fitting place,
the period between Rosh Hashanah and Yom Kippur being
one of divine judgment in Jewish tradition. As elsewhere
in the Gemara, different voices from different times and
places speak in this passage as if coeval and coterminous.
At the outset, mention is made of a controversy between
the House of Shammai, known for its strict interpretations
of law and custom, and the House of Hillel, associated with
less rigorous positions. The House of Shammai, citing the
verse in the biblical book of Zachariah, "And I will bring
the third part through the fire, and will refine them as sil-
ver is refined, and . . . they shall call on my name and I will
hear them," took this to refer to hell and held that

> There are three categories on the day one is judged: the
> totally righteous, the totally sinful, and the intermediate.
> The totally righteous are approved at once for eternal
> life. The totally sinful are condemned at once to Gehen-
> na. . . . The intermediates descend to Gehenna, quake and
> pray [m'tsaftsafim], and ascend again.

The concept of the "intermediate," the person who is
neither all good nor all bad, aligns the rabbis with the
understanding of character in biblical narrative as opposed to the rigid dichotomies of the book of Daniel, the
Pseudepigrapha, and frequently, the prophets. On the face
of it, this makes the House of Shammai unexpectedly

forbearing; for inasmuch as few people are totally righteous or totally sinful, the great majority of souls, it would seem, "quake and pray" in Gehenna and are released quickly. Yet the House of Hillel, we next are told, held that even this was excessive and that the "intermediates" were spared Gehenna entirely. God's *hesed,* His loving mercy, tilts the balance in their favor and admits them immediately to paradise.

Just as we are being impressed by the Talmud's leniency, however, the passage in Rosh Hashanah takes a harsher turn by proceeding to restrict the category of "intermediates" considerably. Inquiring who, according to both first-century schools, is barred from paradise entirely, the text answers anonymously (usually a sign that the view expressed reflects a rabbinical consensus):

> Jews who sin with their bodies and Gentiles who sin with their bodies descend to Gehenna, where they are sentenced to twelve months. When twelve months have passed and nothing is left of the body [in the grave], their souls are burned and the wind scatters their ashes at the feet of the righteous. . . . But Christians and heretics [*minim*], informers, apostates, skeptics who deny the Torah, deniers of the resurrection, strayers from the paths of the community, the intimidators of this world, and those who have not only sinned but have caused others to sin, such as [the biblical figure of] Jeroboam ben Nevat and his associates, descend to Gehenna and are sentenced to remain there forever.

This puts things in a different light. There are, it now seems, numerous souls that are either annihilated completely after the year in Gehenna prescribed by Akiva, like

71

those devoured by the Egyptian "eater of the dead," or condemned to suffer there permanently. The second group includes whoever has openly challenged the belief system of rabbinic Judaism on its own terms, such as Christians and Jewish "heretics," "skeptics," and apostates; any Jew who has defied rabbinic authority by informing on his coreligionists to the Romans or withdrawing from participation in Jewish life; and "the intimidators of this world," identified by the Gemara with the *parnasim,* the wealthy Jewish communal leaders who abuse their money and power for selfish ends. The first group, Jews and Gentiles who "sin with their bodies," Rosh Hashanah explains, comprises Jews "on whose foreheads no phylacteries have lain"—that is, who have failed to perform the physical rituals of Judaism—and Gentiles who, though excused from such rituals, are guilty of "sexual profligacy."

The following exchange now takes place:

A NAMELESS RABBI: "Here, too, the House of Hillel says, 'Loving mercy tilts the balance.'"

A SECOND NAMELESS RABBI: "But who, then [according to the House of Hillel], is referred to by [the verse], 'And I will bring the third part through the fire?'"

FIRST RABBI: "Jews who sin with their bodies."

SECOND RABBI: "Jews who sin with their bodies?! Haven't we just said they are not redeemed [because their souls are annihilated]?"

FIRST RABBI: "They are not redeemed when a majority of their deeds are sinful. If half are sinful and half are not, and the sins include 'sinning with their bodies,' there is no way of avoiding [the verse sentencing them to a term in Gehenna] 'And I will bring the third

part through fire.' But if [they have] not ['sinned with
their bodies'], loving mercy tilts the balance."

In other words, argues the first rabbi, the House of Hillel
maintains that the souls of "intermediate" Jews who have
neglected the rituals of their religion and lived lives that
are more blameworthy than praiseworthy spend twelve
months in Gehenna and are annihilated, whereas the
equally blameworthy and praiseworthy "quake and pray"
in Gehenna and enter paradise, and the more praiseworthy
than blameworthy are exempt from Gehenna altogether.
Furthermore, the more blameworthy, too, are admitted to
paradise at once if they have been ritually observant.

This is the first time in rabbinic tradition that we come
across the idea of our good and bad deeds being weighed
against each other after death—a notion, as old as the ancient Egyptian "scale of truth and justice," that would figure prominently in the Jewish folklore of later ages. In
Rosh Hashanah, it forms part of an attempt to coordi-
nate three different positions: the House of Shammai's, the
House of Hillel's, and a consensus that may have formed
centuries later. The relative unforgivingness of this consensus as compared with earlier views reflects the worsen-
ing vicissitudes of Jewish history.

In the two-hundred-fifty-year period between the
Maccabean revolt and the destruction of the Temple, toward the end of which Hillel and Shammai lived, the overall situation of Jewry in both Palestine and elsewhere in
the Roman empire was good; even after the bloody failures
of the great revolt of 67–70 and the messianically tinged
Bar-Kokhba rebellion of 132–135, Jews continued to enjoy
long periods of calm and prosperity, as they did in the age

f Judah the Prince. It was only after the empire's official adoption of Christianity in the fourth century that its policies, continued in the eastern Mediterranean world by the Byzantines after the fall of Rome in the west, permanently relegated Judaism to the status of a shunned and sometimes hounded religion. A consequence of this was a heightening of vindictive feelings among Jews toward Gentile—now largely Christian—society and Jewish defectors to it. Powerless to retaliate against its enemies in this world, rabbinic Judaism took comfort in the thought of their punishment in the next one.

Even then, however, the Judaism of the Talmudic period never went to the extremes that early Christianity did. Here, for example, is a passage from Tertullian contemplating the fate in hell of the representatives of pagan Rome:

> How vast the spectacle that day, and how wide! What sight shall wake my wonder, what laughter, what joy and exultation, as I see those emperors, those great emperors . . . groaning in the depths of darkness! And the magistrates who persecuted the name of Jesus, liquefying in fiercer flames than they kindled in their rage against Christians! Those sages, too, the philosophers. . . . And the poets trembling before the judgment seat. . . . And the tragic actors to be heard, more vocal in their own tragedy; and the players to be seen, lither of limb by far in the fire; and then the charioteers to watch, red all over in the wheel of flame; and next the athletes to be gazed upon not in their gymnasiums but hurled in the fire.

Nowhere in early rabbinic sources do we find such glee taken in hell's sufferings. True, Tertullian was writing in an age of Christian martyrdom when a desire for vengeance on Christianity's Roman persecutors was natural. But the persecution was not the work of Rome's philosophers, poets, actors, and athletes. Their sin, as far as Tertullian was concerned, was merely their non-Christian lives. Even after Christianity had ceased to be a minority faith rooted in the Jewish sectarianism of the Second Temple period and become the state-endorsed religion of millions, it clung to the sectarian division of humanity into an elect group of the saved and an unregenerate mass of the damned to which God's mercy did not extend.

Such an attitude contrasts strikingly with that of the early rabbis as expressed in another tale about Akiva. This one pits him against a Roman official called by the Talmud "Turnus Rufus"—in reality, Quintus Tinneius Rufus, the Roman governor of Judea whose unpopularity helped spark the Bar-Kokhba rebellion. Akiva and Rufus, it is recounted, once argued about whether the Jewish Sabbath was God-given, and Akiva, to prove his point, told Rufus to visit his father's grave, from which he would see the smoke of hell's fires rising every day except Saturday. Moreover, Akiva predicted, even the most skilled necromancer would be unable to communicate with Rufus' father's soul on the Jewish day of rest. The story concludes:

> At that, Rufus went off and made the test with his father. Every day he raised him [from the dead], but on the Sabbath he could not. After the Sabbath, he again raised him and asked: "Have you become a Jew since you died?" "He who does not observe the Sabbath in your world is not compelled to," replied the father, "but here he must observe it." "What work do you perform on weekdays?"

Rufus asked. "On weekdays," his father answered, "we are punished, but on the Sabbath we are allowed to rest."

This legend takes no interest, let alone pleasure, in the suffering inflicted on the Roman governor's father. What it delights in is the irony of father and son being forced to acknowledge the greater humaneness of Jewish law. Although the Roman upper class, whose slaves and workmen labor seven days a week, scoffs at the Jews for their laziness in taking one of these days off, it will be grateful in Gehenna for the respite this gives it.

And it is only in its moments of respite that Gehenna *can* interest us. Apart from gratifying our vengeful or sadistic emotions, a hell like Tertullian's is every bit as boring to think about as is a heaven like Yehoshua ben Levi's. Both lack the least element of unpredictability or conflict (what conflict between myself and anyone can there be when we are both concerned only with own unbearable pain?) and so cannot speak to our imaginations. These can be engaged only when there are breaks in hell's routine that make room for human intercourse, as in the story of Akiva and Rufus. In itself, there is no more to be gained from the contemplation of never-ending torment than there is from the contemplation of never-ending bliss.

We last left Judah the Prince disputing with Eleazar ben Pedat by the Sea of Galilee. Eleazar was not chosen for this probably fictional dialogue arbitrarily. He was an active figure in a dispute conducted in the Talmudic period between the rabbis of Palestine, who stressed their country's primacy in Jewish life, and those of Babylonia, the other great Jewish center of the times, who argued for a relationship of parity. The Palestinians, the more vocal party, were fighting in a losing cause. From the second century on, Palestinian Jewry gradually waned in numbers and influence while the Jewish community of Babylonia prospered and grew. Life in Babylonia was better. Its Jews, generally well treated by their rulers, rarely encountered the political oppression and religious persecution that Jews faced in Roman and Byzantine Palestine.

It was in the context of this dispute that Eleazar attacked Diaspora Jews who sought to reap the benefits of burial in the Land of Israel. Moreover, basing himself on the prophet Joel's description of the last judgment being held in the Valley of Jehoshaphat, at the foot of Jerusalem's Mount of Olives, he asserted that only in the Land of Israel would the resurrection that followed judgment day take place. "The dead outside the land do not live again," the Gemara's tractate of Ketubot quotes him as saying with the help of a creatively interpreted verse from Ezekiel. If one cannot afford to have one's remains transported to a burial site like Bet-She'arim, one had better live and die in God's promised land.

At once Eleazar is challenged in the Gemara by his fellow Tiberian, Rabbi Abba bar Memel, who cites a verse from Isaiah in support of the opposite view. Confronted by Eleazar with still another verse, however, Abba bar Memel makes a partial concession. There is indeed, he grants, a difference between the Land of Israel and elsewhere; it does not, however, concern Jews, who will rise from the grave everywhere. Rather, in the Land of Israel, "even a Canaanite maidservant is promised the world-to-come."

Those who will be resurrected there alone are the deserving Gentiles.

"But does this mean, according to Rabbi Eleazar, that righteous Jews outside the Land of Israel will not come to life again?" the Talmud asks in a startled tone. A way of avoiding such a radical conclusion is now suggested by Rabbi Il'a, who also studied in Tiberias with Yohanan bar Nafha. Eleazar's intention, he proposes, is to rule out, not the resurrection of righteous Jews from the Diaspora, but their resurrection *in* the Diaspora. On judgment day, their bones will travel to the Land of Israel by "tumbling" to it (*al y'dey gilgul*), after which they, too, will have their souls restored.

"But this will cause the righteous pain!" objects another rabbi. At this point, the great Babylonian sage Abayey steps in. "Tunnels [*mehilot*] will be made for them," he explains. Traveling safely through these underground highways, the bones of the righteous will reach the Holy Land unscathed.

As with early rabbinic descriptions of heaven and hell, it is difficult to say how much of all this was meant to be taken at face value. Talmudic discourse often has a playfulness that is engaged in for its own sake without thought of its reception by later ages. Yet later ages granted this passage the same authority as any other in the Talmud, and *gilgul mehilot,* the underground locomotion of bones to the Land of Israel, became a widespread Jewish belief. Although burial in the holy land remained an ideal, so that a scattering of Jews throughout the ages either went there to die or requested to be interred there after death, the belief that the dead traveled to Jerusalem by tunnel on judgment day took hold in the Jewish imagination.

I try to picture it. All I can think of is the noise. At first it's an irregular clatter as the ground opens beneath my grave and my bones chute into a sloping passageway barely large enough to crawl through and begin tumbling down it. Bones from other graves join them as the grave-yard rapidly empties out.

The noise grows louder. Ahead is a sound like the rattle of a train. The tunnel is entered by another, and bones from a second graveyard hurtle into it. Bone knocks against bone. Bone sends bone flying. My forearm is caught in someone's pelvis. Someone's vertebrae ride on my skull. The bones jostle along their underground route.

More and more tunnels feed into it. Or else it debouches into them. It's now high enough to stand in. The bones roar through it like a river in flood. For hours, days, they pursue their downward course. Only one place on earth is low enough to receive them.

The Sea of Salt!

The bones spatter onto the Dead Sea's shores from the base of the barren hills around it. They lie piled by the water's edge. They spread over the alluvial fans of the dry wadis. They litter the banks of the Jordan where it enters the sea's northern end. They are heaped, everywhere, like seashells swept ashore by a storm.

Can they live?

Lord God, Thou knowest.

The question is God's. The answer is Ezekiel's. God says to him:

Prophesy upon these bones, and say unto them: O ye dry bones, hear the word of the Lord! Behold, I will cause the breath to enter into you, and ye shall live. And I will lay

79

sinews upon you, and will bring up flesh upon you, and cover you with skin, and put breath in you, and ye shall live; and ye shall know that I am the Lord.

Then,

I prophesied as I was commanded; and as I prophesied, there was a noise, and behold a shaking, and the bones came together, bone to bone. And when I beheld, lo, the sinews and the flesh came upon them, and the skin covered them above; but there was no breath in them. Then he said unto me, Prophesy unto the wind, prophesy, son of man, and say to the wind, Thus saith the Lord God: Come from the four winds, O breath, and breathe upon these slain that they may live. So I prophesied as he commanded me, and the breath came upon them, and they lived, and stood up upon their feet, an exceeding great army.

I stretch out an arm. It's mine. A leg. Sore but my own. I take a step, lose my balance, regain it.

Around me, pandemonium. Bewildered, I sit on the ground. Where, in this great crowd of refugees from the grave, do I begin looking for anyone?

Four thousand feet above me, to the west, rises the Mount of Olives.

The early rabbis understood the absurdity, to a rational mind, of human beings coming back to life in their original bodies long after their deaths. Their belief that this was possible came down to the belief that nothing for God was impossible. They expressed this, as they did most ideas, by narrative, metaphor, and exegesis rather than philosophical reasoning, their most sustained discussion of the topic occurring in a long chapter of the Gemara's tractate of Sanhedrin, which comments on a shorter chapter on the resurrection in the Mishnaic tractate of the same name.

A story in Sanhedrin tells of a supposed conversation between Rabbi Gamaliel I, the great-great-grandfather of Judah the Prince, and an unnamed Roman emperor and his daughter. The emperor asks how, life having returned to dust, dust can return to life again, and before Gamaliel can answer, the emperor's daughter answers for him. Think, she tells her father, of two potters, one making his pots from moistened clay and one from liquid alone: which is the more accomplished? "The one who makes them from liquid alone," the emperor replies, knowing no such potter exists. "If God, then, creates a man from pure liquid," his daughter rejoins, alluding to the drop of sperm that the ancients thought was the sole material cause of conception, "cannot He create one from clay?"

What is unusual about this story is not its parable, which resembles others of its kind in Talmudic literature, but its speaker. If even an aristocratic Roman woman, the inference is, considers a belief in resurrection to be reasonable, there is no dismissing it as mere Jewish credulity. Were the story a true one, its emperor would have had to have been Domitian, Trajan, or Hadrian in order to be Gamaliel's contemporary. Perhaps the figure of the daughter was suggested by Domitian and Trajan's female cousin Domitilla, who was known to have been attracted to Judaism.

Of course, many of the conundrums that apply to the first, heavenly stage of the afterlife apply to its second, earthly stage as well. When the dead rise, what aspect and age of themselves will they be? If we die old or disabled, will we rise young and robust? If so, what happens to that part of our selves that postdates our infirmity? If not, what is the point of rising? And once risen, will we proceed to die again? Suppose we will: does this mean we will come back to life over and over, ad infinitum? Suppose we won't: will we then go on growing older and older forever?

In the same passage in Sanhedrin, Shim'on ben Lakish answers the first set of questions by comparing two verses from the Bible, both assumed to refer to the messianic age and the resurrection. One is Jeremiah 31:8: "Behold, I will gather them from the ends of the earth, the blind and the lame, the woman with child and her that travaileth with child." The other is Isaiah 35:56: "Then the eyes of the blind shall be made clear and the ears of the deaf shall be unstopped; then shall the lame man leap as a gazelle and the tongue of the dumb sing." Taken together, Ben-Lakish says, these verses mean that the dead "will rise with their infirmities and be cured." We will be resurrected in the condition we died in and only then be restored to full health.

This view is echoed in Genesis Rabba, where it is stated: "As one departs [from this world], so will one return. Whoever departs blind will return blind; whoever departs deaf will return deaf; whoever departs dumb will return dumb." If we die young, we will rise young; if old, old. We will not even have a change of clothes. When asked, according to the Talmud, by another reputed royal admirer of Judaism, the Egyptian queen Cleopatra, whether the dead would come back to life naked, Rabbi Meir replied: "Learn from a grain of wheat. If it is buried [i.e., sown] naked but sprouts fully clothed [in its husks], how much more so will the righteous who are buried in their garments rise in them."

The second set of questions is answered by Ulla, a Palestinian sage who also studied in Tiberias but spent much of his time in Babylonia before dying there. (Hearing that his bones were on their way to the Land of Israel for burial, his acquaintance Eleazar characteristically remarked, "Being taken in by the land after living [in it] is not like being taken in after dying [somewhere else].") Citing Isaiah 25:8, "He will swallow up death in victory," and Isaiah 65:20, "No more shall there be [in messianic times] a man who has not lived out his days, for each child shall die one hundred years old," Ulla observes that dying at one hundred is nevertheless dying; where, then, is the victory over death? He then resolves the difficulty by explaining that the first verse refers to Jews, the second to Gentiles. The resurrected Jew will live forever. The resurrected Gentile will die at a ripe old age.

Ulla agrees, then, with Abba bar Memel that some Gentiles will be resurrected. So also, it would appear, does the Mishnaic tractate of Sanhedrin, which begins:

All Israel has a place in the world-to-come, for it is written [Isaiah, 60:21], "Thy people are all righteous, they shall inherit the land forever." But the following do not have a place: whoever denies the God-givenness of the Torah and the existence of resurrection, and the adherent of Greek philosophy [epikoros]. . . . Three kings and four commoners [mentioned in the Bible] have no place in the world-to-come. The three kings are Jeroboam, Ahab, and Menasseh. . . . The four commoners are Bilam, Doeg, Ahitophel, and Gehazi.

Although this mishnah differs in its categories from the tractate of Rosh Hashanah, according to which not only heretics and skeptics but some ritually unobservant Jews, too, fail to emerge from Gehenna, both agree that most Jews will rise from the dead. As for Gentiles, they are not, at first glance, mentioned by the mishnah—but look again. In its list of the four "commoners" denied resurrection because of their wickedness, only the last three are Israelites; the first, Bilam, is described by the book of Numbers as an Aramean sorcerer hired by the king of Moab to put a curse on Israel. And the Gemara comments on this: "If Bilam does not enter the world-to-come, [this must mean that] others [who are Gentiles] do." For if that weren't the case, why single Bilam out?

An exchange now takes place between the xenophobic Eleazar and the more open Yehoshua ben Levi. (Yehoshua's greater tolerance of non-Jews is conveyed in the Talmud by a story about how once, on the verge of swearing at an obnoxious Christian, he thought of the verse from Psalms, "His mercy is on all His creatures," and held his tongue.) Eleazar objects to this interpretation of the mishnah, citing another verse from Psalms, "The wicked shall return to She'ol and all the nations forgetful of God." By "the wicked," he asserts, the Psalmist designates sinful Jews who will not be resurrected; by "all the nations forgetful of God," every last Gentile. Yehoshua disagrees. "The wicked" and "all the nations forgetful of God," he declares, are one and the same. Gentiles who have been mindful of God and have sought to live by His precepts, even if not within the framework of Judaism, are not wicked and will rise from the grave, too.

Eleazar and Yehoshua represent the two poles of unqualified rejection and qualified acceptance of the Gentile world that have done battle with each other throughout Jewish history. A third position, closer in attitude to Eleazar's, is taken by Ulla. When asked by a supporter of Eleazar why Gentiles would be needed in the world-to-come, Ulla answers with yet another quotation, this time from Isaiah: "And strangers shall stand and feed your flocks and the sons of foreigners shall be your plowmen and your vine-dressers." After the resurrection, Israel's work will be done for it by others. Abba bar Memel's "Canaanite maidservant" will be part of this workforce.

And yet she will not have to work very hard, for life after the resurrection, we are promised by Sanhedrin, will be transformed. Each stalk of wheat will grow to be as tall as a palm tree—nor will reaping it be a problem, since the wind will cause its kernels, each as large as the kidney of an ox, to rain down. One stalk will feed an entire family. A single grape vine will yield an amphora of wine. Every tree will bear edible fruit all year long and the earth will bring forth cakes and fine woolens. God will hold a great banquet for the righteous and serve them Leviathan and mammoth meat.

Such hyperboles call for more than a grain of salt. Clearly, however, the early rabbis agreed that the risen dead would eat and drink as their souls did not necessarily do in heaven. They would have sex and procreate, too. (How else could children who live to be one hundred be born?) The difference between the heavenly afterlife and the earthly one is that on earth we get back our real bodies, not just facsimiles of them—and these will have actual stomachs that hunger and actual loins that feel desire. Anything less would be a sham.

But will not life after the resurrection, then, have the same conflicts that life would have in heaven were we to possess our full physical natures there? Although there is no explicit discussion of this question in Talmudic literature, there is an implied one in an unlikely place. This is the Talmudic tractate of Nidah, which deals with laws of menstrual impurity. A halakhic digression in it goes:

> If a garment has [a segment of] mixed fabrics that cannot be located, one must not sell it to a Gentile or use it for a donkey's saddlebag, but one may use it for a shroud for the dead. Rabbi Yosef asked, "Are the commandments then annulled in the world-to-come?" He was answered by Abayey, "This [permission to clothe the dead in such a garment] applies only to when they are being eulogized [before burial], but it is forbidden to bury them in it". . . . Rabbi Yohanan says, "[It is permissible] even to bury them in it." Rabbi Yohanan was being true to his principles, for he [also] said [citing part of a verse from Psalms], " 'Free among the dead'—once a man dies, he is free of the commandments."

This passage demands to be read closely. Since there is a biblical commandment forbidding the interweaving of two different fabrics like linen and wool, a garment made of such a mixture must be discarded. On the other hand, if only a part of the garment is mixed, one may rip this part out and use the remainder. But what if it can't be ripped out because, though its existence is known, its exact location in the garment is not? In that case, we are told, the entire garment is forbidden, even for use as a saddlebag. The one exception is its use as a shroud.

Such is the agreed-on law. But since it is also agreed that the dead will rise in the clothes they were buried in, whoever is resurrected in such a shroud, Rabbi Yosef points out, will be in violation of the biblical commandment. Does this mean the commandments will cease to be in force after the resurrection? Abayey thinks it doesn't and gives a rather strained justification of his opinion. (Why would anyone be eulogized in one shroud and buried in another?) Yohanan thinks it does and defends his view with a quote from Psalms.

Yohanan's use of this quote, it must be said, is farfetched, too; rather than referring to the resurrection, the verse he quotes from would seem to deny its very existence. (In full it reads: "I am as a man that has no strength, free among the dead like the slain in the grave whom Thou rememberest no more.") Moreover, the entire discussion has little relationship to any conceivable reality. What are the chances of anyone's being buried in a shroud known to have an unlocatable mixture of fabrics?

But this is the way the Talmud often works, choosing low-probability situations to generate high-interest questions. And the question being asked here has to do, it would seem, with the rabbinic concepts of *yetser ha-tov* and *yetser ha-ra*, the good and evil inclinations, the perpetual struggle between which determines human conduct. In a resurrected humanity from which economic scarcity and competition have been banished by a miraculously bounteous nature, will the evil inclination still be active, so that we continue to need divine laws and regulations to curb our behavior? Or will it be permanently overcome, enabling us to resolve most differences spontaneously by being naturally good and cooperative?

The argument about mixed fabrics is thus an argument about human nature. Abayey, it can be assumed, believes the evil inclination to be intractable; without the code of the Torah to keep it in check, mankind will lapse into savagery even in the world-to-come. Yohanan holds that in a more plentiful world the good inclination will prevail, thus eliminating the necessity for outer constraints.

Such a dispute lies at the heart of all debates between utopian and anti-utopian visions of the future. For the one, evil is a product of social and economic circumstance; for the other, it is ineradicably rooted in who we are. Did Cain kill Abel because men are born with murderous instincts? Then "Thou shalt not kill" will have to be rigorously inculcated in us even when we are resurrected. Did he do so only because, being a farmer rather than a shepherd, he was driven to a lethal fit of jealousy by the inferior sacrifice he was made to offer? Such situations will no longer exist when we rise from the dead. Not until then will we know whether human life can be fundamentally different while still remaining human or whether, even when lasting forever, it must go on being essentially the same.

CHAPTER THREE

ALTHOUGH A BELIEF IN THE AFTERLIFE'S TWO STAGES remained central in Judaism up to modern times, the two were not as a rule equally stressed. In the early centuries of the Common Era, when messianic expectations remained strong despite rabbinic attempts to steer them away from politically dangerous expression, the resurrection was emphasized more. The second of the "eighteen benedictions" in the Amidah or Shemoneh Esreh prayer, which dates to this period and climaxes each of the three daily services, thanks God for "keeping faith with all who sleep in the dust" and ends, "Blessed art Thou O Lord, who bringest the dead back to life." There is nothing similar in early Jewish liturgy regarding the disembodied soul's fate after death.

Yet as time went by, messianic hopes, while continuing to coalesce sporadically around this or that event or figure in the Jewish world, gradually lost their power of immediacy for most Jews. They were dealt a severe blow by the crushing of the Bar-Kokhba rebellion. They were disappointed again in the year 363, when the Roman emperor Flavius Claudius Julianus, better known by his Christian name of Julian the Apostate, ordered the Temple rebuilt in Jerusalem as part of his campaign to de-Christianize the

Roman Empire; begun to feverish Jewish excitement, the work ended suddenly when Julian died in battle and the empire reverted to a pro-Christian course. Hopes soared and collapsed once more in 614, after the capture of Jerusalem from the Byzantines by a Persian army in which many Jews fought. A Jewish governor was appointed to rule the city, plans were laid for a third Temple, and biblical sacrifice was reinstituted. Yet the governor was soon murdered and Jerusalem was retaken by the Byzantines, only to fall a few years later to the Muslim forces that stormed out of Arabia following the death of Muhammad. Not until modern times was the dream of a Jewish restoration in the Land of Israel once again to have any perceivable basis in reality.

The Islamic conquest of the Middle East, North Africa, and Spain, besides ending the Talmudic period, has been viewed by historians as marking the onset of the Middle Ages—and medieval Jews, in thinking about death and the afterlife, thought less on the whole about resurrection and more about heaven and hell. The first now seemed a distant prospect. The other awaited them soon.

This shift of emphasis took place over time. One effect of the Muslim environment in which most of the world's Jews now lived was the emergence, under the impact of Islamic thought (itself deeply influenced by the thought of the Greeks), of a body of Jewish religious philosophy, much of it written in Arabic, such as had not existed in antiquity. Dedicated to demonstrating that Judaism was consistent with human reason, its first prominent representative was the tenth-century Sa'adia Ga'on, head of the great Babylonian yeshiva of Sura. On the face of it, Sa'adia's major work, *The Book of Beliefs and Opinions*, equates the world-to-come almost exclusively with the resurrection.

The soul and body, it maintains, cannot function without each other in a next life any more than they can in this one. Until their reunion, the souls of the dead will be preserved in a kind of suspended animation, those of the righteous apart from those of the wicked, much as is described in parts of Enoch I.

Sa'adia begins his discussion of resurrection by dealing with the objections to it, not by parable and metaphor as do the rabbis of the Talmud, but by an attempt at scientific analysis. One common caveat, he writes, is that the risen bodies of the dead, if recomposed from their original earth, water, fire, and air, the four elements believed by medieval science to form the basis of all matter, would need to include substances that had also been in other bodies. Thus, for instance, every breath a person takes may include particles of air that have been breathed by someone else before him and released from that person's decomposed body after death, or for that matter, from any number of bodies. To whom will these particles belong on the day of the resurrection? And how could anyone deprived of them rise as a complete human being if components of him are missing?

In rebuttal, Sa'adia enlists the astronomy of his times. Science has determined, he observes, that the distance from the earth to the heavens is 1,089 times the earth itself.[1] Since all of this vast space is filled with air, which circulates constantly, it is reasonable to assume that no

---

1   Sa'adia's actual language is that this distance is 1,089 times "the entire earth." Presumably, he is referring to medieval calculations of the distance from the earth to the sun based on multiples of the earth's radius, but even then it is not clear where his figure of 1,089, or 33 squared, comes from. The closest I have found to it in the science of his time is that of 1,108 earth radii, given by the Arab astronomer Abu Abdullah al-Battan.

person ever breathes the same air that was part of another person's body. In the resurrection, therefore, each body will have restored to it the air that belonged to it alone.

Sa'adia also resorts to arithmetical calculations in dealing with the contention that were all the Jewish dead to rise from their graves, the earth would have no room for them. Taking an average human life-span to be the Bible's threescore-and-ten years, he posits thirty-two such spans for the 2,400 years of Israelite history from the Exodus to his own age. Suppose, he says, that 1,200,000 Israelites lived in each span.[2] If every single one of them were resurrected, their number would not exceed 38,400,000. Should this population inhabit 360,000 square miles of territory, which is less than one hundred-fiftieth of the surface of the earth,[3] each Israelite could be allotted nearly a hundredth of a square mile—or by Sa'adia's reckoning, 288 square cubits of land, the equivalent of six-and-a-half modern acres. This would be more than enough for a family to live on while raising crops and cattle. But for Sa'adia even this much is unnecessary, since there will be no crops or cattle in the world-to-come. There will indeed be little there that we are accustomed to, since

2   This is based on the biblical number of 600,000 Israelites leaving Egypt, which Sa'adia assumes to be the size of a Jewish generation throughout history. Allowing thirty-five years for each generation, he arrives at two generations, or 600,000 × 2, in every seventy-year span.
3   A medieval Arab mile was 10–20 percent longer than a modern one, and Sa'adia was apparently thinking of God's promise to Abraham in the book of Genesis that his descendants would inherit all the land from the frontier of Egypt to the Euphrates River. Such an area, which would include today's Sinai Peninsula, Palestine, Transjordan, and Syria, comprises approximately 330,000 modern square miles—which, multiplied by 150, yields a total planetary land surface of 50 million square miles. This is not far from the actual figure of 57 million.

the earth [as we know it] is designed for the produc-
tion of food, which is why there are gardens, and fields
for planting, and rivers and streams for watering trees
and livestock, and seas for [providing water vapor for]
rain, and prairies for animals to graze in, and roads to
travel on. We require these things in this world for food
and trade, but in the world-to-come there will be neither food nor trade, and no need for fields, plants, rivers,
streams, and the like.

The very air will be different and more salubrious, so that
breathing it alone will nourish the body. Not even the sky
will be the same: the sun will no longer rise and set, and
there will be perpetual light. What purpose would darkness serve? In the world we inhabit now, Sa'adia explains,
"our days are for business and earning a livelihood and our
nights are for rest, quiet, reflection, sexual activity, and the
like. But there will be none of this [i.e., commerce or sex] in
the world to-come and no need for day and night."

Such an earth reminds one of Rav's heaven. Its inhabitants, too, do little but bathe in a divine radiance in which
they are permanently immersed. The sole difference is that
they have real bodies—which, however, being scarcely
used, are largely unnecessary. This was Sa'adia's way of
solving a dilemma. On the one hand, he was committed by
his belief in the divine origin of Scripture to the biblical
Daniel's prophecy of the dead rising from their graves. On
the other hand, besides being aware, like Rav, of the necessarily imperfect nature of a world-to-come in which normal physical functions are retained, he ranked the physical life below the mental one on his scale of philosophical
values. By treating the afterlife's second, embodied stage as

if it were its first, disembodied one and in effect merging the two, he dodged the difficulty.

A more radical approach was that of the twelfth-century Maimonides, known to Jewish tradition as "the Rambam," an acronym for Rabbi Moshe ben Maimon. A towering figure in both philosophy and rabbinics, and the court physician in Cairo to Saladin and other sultans, he carried Sa'adia's rationalism even farther by reversing the afterlife's two stages. The resurrection, he maintained in a treatise on it and in a commentary on the discussion of it in Sanhedrin, is not the final, climactic phase of the world-to-come. Although the dead will rise as prophesied, they will proceed to live ordinary lives like those we live now and to die once more at the end of them. There will continue to be rich and poor and strong and weak among them, and apart from their coming to life again, which is a divine miracle that must be accepted (somewhat reluctantly on Maimonides' part, one feels) as a dogma of Judaism, the laws of nature and human behavior will remain unchanged.

The culmination of the world-to-come, Maimonides believed, lay in the bodiless soul's immortality. His notion of this immortality, however, was so abstract that Rav's heaven is almost vivid by comparison. The "only source of eternal life," Maimonides writes in his great philosophical work *A Guide for the Perplexed*, is "knowledge," whether "arrived at by speculation or established by research," and it is only as "an intelligent being [which] knows about the things in existence everything that a perfectly developed person is capable of knowing" that the soul survives after death.

If such a formulation seems opaque, this is because Maimonides, well aware that his conception of the afterlife would have little attraction for the average Jew, preferred it to be. As in much of the *Guide*, his views must be pieced together, like the parts of a puzzle, from seemingly unrelated passages—in one of which elsewhere he defines what "knowledge" is. ""When the intellect comprehends a thing," he writes there, it is "not a thing distinct from the thing comprehended." If, for example, we have knowledge of a tree that is more than a fleeting sensory perception of this or that pine tree or palm tree,

> the thing comprehended is the abstract form of the tree, and at the same time it is the intellect in action; and the intellect and the abstract form of the tree are not two different things, for the intellect in action is nothing but the thing comprehended and that agent by which the form of the tree has been turned into an intellectual and abstract object. . . . The intellect, that which comprehends, and that which is comprehended are therefore the same whenever a real comprehension takes place.

It is this "intellect in action" that is eternal life's "only source": not the memory of a particular tree that has been seen, but a comprehension, arrived at by philosophical or scientific thought, of the "treeness" that makes every tree a tree rather than, say, a stalk or a bush; and since such abstract knowledge, insofar as it is accurate, will be the same for any two individuals, the immortal soul of Individual A will be no different in respect of it from the immortal soul of Individual B. The two will diverge only in terms of how much knowledge of this sort they have amassed—so that if A, let us say, has mastered no more than addition and subtraction while B has also studied trigonometry, more of B's soul will survive after death in the laws of mathematics.

It will not do so, however, as a self-conscious being with an identity of its own. It will simply live on in the eternal truths it has comprehended—or to put it differently, these truths will perpetuate it to the extent, and only to the extent, that they have been correctly understood by it.

Although Maimonides wished to conceal his disbelief in personal immortality from those who lacked, in his opinion, the intellectual maturity to cope with it, he would have denied that this was heretical from a Jewish point of view. In his "Thirteen Articles of Faith," which is the closest thing to an authoritative creed that Judaism has, resurrection is included while heaven and hell, which he did not believe to have a scriptural basis, are not. To be sure, Article Eleven affirms the existence of divine "reward and punishment" for one's deeds. Yet all this meant for Maimonides was that the philosophically lived life, whatever its tribulations, is its own recompense by virtue of the peace of mind it brings, just as the life lived in pursuit of material goods and pleasures, which inevitably leads to unhappiness, is its own retribution. In all of this, he pushed logical thought to the limit—well beyond what most Jews might have taken comfort in.

Its inability to speak to the common Jew left Judaism's alliance with philosophy, though one of the great intellectual projects of medieval Jewish life, without significant impact on popular religion. When it came to ordinary notions of death and the afterlife, this alliance rationalized them when it could and dismissed them when it couldn't. Sa'adia, for example, describes a belief, widespread in his day, in what was known in Hebrew as *hibbut ha-kever*, "the thrashing of the grave," according to which the freshly interred dead are beaten for their sins by avenging angels even before undergoing divine judgment. A medieval text on the subject relates that as soon as anyone is buried, the Angel of Death commands him or her, "Rise and tell me your name!" Disoriented by their new surroundings, the dead reply, "God knows I can't remember it," and the angel proceeds to strike them limb by limb with an iron chain. They are beaten around the eyes for having failed to discern the truth; upon the ears for listening to idle talk; on the mouth for having borne false witness; across the legs for hurrying to commit sins; and so on. This continues until the skeleton falls apart.

Rather than reject the notion of *hibbut ha-kever* outright as gross superstition, Sa'adia seeks to explain it as a misunderstanding of a natural process. After its separation from its body at death, he writes,

> the soul remains agitatedly nearby until the body has decomposed. This decomposition is hard for it because it knows what is being done to the body by worms, maggots, and the like, just as it is hard for a man to see the house he has lived in fall into ruins and be overgrown with weeds. . . . This is what is called the judgment or thrashing of the grave.

But other new beliefs about the afterlife that had begun to spread in Sa'adia's day were condemned by him categorically. One of them involved reincarnation. "There are those calling themselves Jews," he writes,

> among whom, I must say, I have encountered the idea of transmigration of souls, which holds that the soul of

Reuben will return [to earth after his death] as Simon, and then as Levi, and then as Judah. Many even profess that a human soul can be [reborn] in an animal, or an animal soul in a human, as well as similarly mad and confused notions.

So foreign to Judaism does this idea seem to Sa'adia that he does not bother to present a proper philosophical refutation of it. (Nor, given its acceptance by the Greek Neoplatonists, would he have found it easy to come up with one.) He simply observes that it lacks all scriptural authority; that it was borrowed by Jews from Manicheans and Christian Gnostics; that its explanation that we suffer in this life because of our soul's sins in a past one is rendered superfluous by the Jewish doctrine of reward and punishment in the world-to-come; and that it is absurd to think that a human soul could be joined to an animal's body. Body and soul compose a single entity, and neither has the power to humanize or dehumanize the other. This, Sa'adia says, would be "contrary to all that is intelligible."

Sa'adia's discussion of reincarnation may be the earliest medieval reference to a Jewish belief in it. Besides having been taken from Manicheans and Christian Gnostics, two religious groups with strength in the eastern Islamic world in which Sa'adia lived, such a belief may also have been influenced by religions farther to the east, such as Hinduism and Buddhism. Nor is it impossible that it was passed down for centuries in oral form from Jewish Neoplatonist circles like Philo's.

An actual endorsement of reincarnation first surfaces in Jewish sources long after Sa'adia's age, in the *Sefer ha-Bahir* or "Book of Clarity," an influential pre- or early kabbalistic text. While the *Bahir*'s provenance is murky, it was most likely composed in the twelfth century in southern France, which would put it close to the Christian heresy of Catharism that flourished in the region at the time and that affirmed the transmigration of souls, too. In one passage, the *Bahir* asks the ancient question "Why do the wicked prosper and the righteous suffer?" and gives an unconventional Jewish answer: "Because the righteous were wicked in [other lives in] the past and are now being punished for it."

The passage goes on to observe that although the Torah, as stated by the verse in Psalms "He commanded His word to the thousandth generation," was meant to be given to Moses at Mount Sinai a thousand generations after the creation of humanity, the actual number of generations from Adam to Moses is only twenty-six. What happened to the other 974? God, the *Bahir* says, destroyed them for their wickedness and created human beings again time after time, each time recycling their souls, which were gradually purged of evil. This continued until the generation of Adam, when righteousness first appeared. Even then, however, many souls had yet to pay their full debt from previous incarnations and went on being afflicted by misfortune when reborn in new bodies.

A belief in reincarnation augmented Judaism with yet another way of thinking about life after death—one that, latecomer though it was, would take its place as a near equal alongside the older conceptions. It did so at first semi-surreptitiously since, lacking any basis in the Bible or Talmud, it was not easily defended. Most commonly, it was claimed to be ancient esoteric knowledge that had never been committed to writing. The thirteenth-century Nahmanides (known as "the Ramban," an acronym for Rabbi Moshe ben Nahman) refers to it cryptically in his commentary on the book of Genesis as "a great secret of the Torah" that is revealed to "whomever God has given eyes to see and ears to hear." He does this while writing about the story of Judah, whose son Onan shirked his father's command to impregnate Tamar, the widow of Onan's brother Er, because "he knew the seed would not be his." Since the physical seed *would* be his, this could only mean, the Ramban hints, that Onan realized that any child born to Tamar would have his brother's soul. This was a "mystery" imparted to Onan by his father Judah, who had received it from his ancestors, and it continued to be transmitted from generation to generation until made public by the author of *Sefer ha-Bahir.*

It's poignant, Sa'adia's image of the soul lingering by its body like a man, evicted from the house he has lived in, who stays in the neighborhood to watch it fall apart. Only when he has lost all hope of being able to move back in does he agree to start a new life elsewhere.

I like the comparison. I, too, would feel homeless without my body. And yet, doesn't the very word "I" defeat my meaning? For if "I" am, as Sa'adia says, a fusion of body and soul, how can I call my bodiless soul "I"?

I get up from the desk I am writing at and pace my study. My study is small, made smaller by the bookcases that leave little room for pacing. There's no more room in them for books, either. Books are stacked on the floor. Books are piled on the easy chair I've stopped sitting in because they've taken my place there. Books line the shelves I've built in the attic. Each time I pass through its low doorway to look for one, I risk bumping my head.

I pace: from the two large windows by my desk to the stairs descending to the ground floor and back again. My study is the only room on the second floor. It rises above the rest of the house, one window looking northwest, over the roof toward the sea, which I once had a glimpse of before the neighbors' trees hid it, the other northeast, into the range of the Carmel. From the desk to the stairs is six strides. From the stairs to the desk is six strides the other way.

I pace and think: what is this thought that I am thinking? It is about bodies and souls, but it is also about the scrape of my sandals on the wooden floor, the pain in the tendon of the heel that I sprained a week ago, the ache in my back from sitting too long at my desk, the August light pouring through the northeast window, the old sheet I hang there every April to keep out the morning sun as it progresses northward on its way to the summer solstice and take down again in September when it has retreated far enough to the south. Each time I reach the stairs and turn back, I see this sheet. Its shabbiness annoys me and I think: for years I've been promising myself to replace it with a Venetian blind and I've never done it. Soon I'll be dead and there'll be no need to do anything.

I suppose Maimonides would say that the only real knowledge in any of this that will survive me is what I know about the summer solstice, but right now I don't give a damn for Maimonides. The laws of nature interest me less than the pain in my heel. How will my soul get along without its body? It's used to it. It's shaped and been shaped by it. Why would it want another, even if it could have one? Nothing would fit. We wouldn't be me. It would be like sleeping with a strange woman instead of with my wife. Yes, I know: there are couples who stay married for long years, are happy together, never think of leaving each other—and then one of them dies and the other grieves and gets over it and marries again. More power to him or her, but this strikes me as promiscuous. My soul has never wanted another body and never will.

I return to my desk and write: *the absurdity of resurrection—the only hope.*

❧

Reincarnation and marriage figure together in the Zohar, or "Book of Splendor," too.

The Zohar is the seminal text of Kabbalah, which was the second major intellectual enterprise of the Jewish Middle Ages and a rebellion against philosophy. The only Jewish book to have been accorded (although not by all Jews) a sacredness like the Bible's and the Talmud's, and second only to them in its historical influence on Jewish thought, the Zohar purports to be the work of the ascetic second-century Mishnaic sage Shim'on bar Yohai. Its actual author, the late thirteenth-century Spanish kabbalist Moshe de Leon, wrote it in Aramaic, the language of the Talmud that Middle Eastern Jews stopped using when they switched to Arabic after the spread of Islam, in order to present it as an ancient manuscript that had come into his possession. To this day, kabbalistic tradition holds de Leon's account to be true, even though his wife confessed soon after his death that such a manuscript never existed.

Although the Zohar borrows freely from mystical Jewish texts that preceded it, such as the *Bahir*, it is a thoroughly original composition. A long, rambling work taking the form of a commentary on each of the weekly portions of the Pentateuch, it aspires to be nothing less than an anatomy of God and an anthropology of the human soul, the different parts of each of which participate in a great cosmic drama. Indeed, that God *has* different parts— that, far from being the perfect unity that philosophers like Sa'adia and Maimonides understood Him to be, He unfolds by means of emanations called Sefirot, dynamic and sometimes dangerously contending forces that are continually in and out of balance—was the Zohar's revolutionary contribution to Judaism. It is the Jew's task, the Zohar holds, to help maintain this balance, and to restore it when it is disturbed, by keeping the Torah's commandments with the proper spiritual intent.

As did Neoplatonism and Gnosticism, the Zohar conceives of the soul as preexisting the body. Unlike them, however, it does not believe that the soul chooses to inhabit the body foolishly or is made to do so by an evil force. Rather, when God created the world,

> He made all the souls that were destined to be given to human beings in future times. . . . When its time comes, God summons each soul and says to it, "Go, get you to such-and-such a place and such-and-such a body." The soul replies: "Master of the Universe, the world I am in now is enough for me. I don't want to go to another

world in which I will be sullied and enslaved." God says: "From the day you were created, you were created to be in that world." When the soul sees this is so, it goes forth and descends against its will. The Torah, the world's counselor, sees how it [the descended soul] lights the way for the world's inhabitants and says to them, "See what mercy God has on you. He has given His precious pearl to you as a gift."

The soul has its divine mission. If it performs that mission well, it returns to its heavenly home when its time in the body is over. If it doesn't, it may be sentenced to the punishments of Gehenna—or, more rarely in the Zohar, to reincarnation in another body. The Zohar calls this *gilgul*, the same word encountered in the phrase *gilgul mehilot*, the tumbling through tunnels of the bones of the dead. Deriving from *galgal*, "wheel," it can also mean a cycle—in this case, the cycle of birth, death, and rebirth.

The most memorable discussion of *gilgul* in the Zohar is known as that of "the Old Man of Mishpatim." Given a fictional, Mishnaic setting like many of the Zohar's homilies, it takes the form of an extended monologue delivered by an elderly donkey driver who has pretended to the rabbi he is traveling with to be a garrulous bore when he is in fact a man of hidden wisdom. His words are a mystical explication of the opening verses of the Torah reading of Mishpatim in the book of Exodus (21:2–21:12), which lay down the laws of bondage and release from it. "If thou buy a Hebrew slave," the first of these laws reads, "six years shall he serve, and in the seventh he shall go out free for nothing."

One of the concerns of Mishpatim is the status in such an arrangement of women, such as a female bondservant married to a slave who is freed in the seventh year by his master, and from this the old man weaves an elaborate parable in which the master is God and the slave and bondservant are male and female souls. Commenting on the next verse, "If he [the slave] came in [to his master's service] alone, he shall go forth alone; if he has a wife, his wife shall go forth with him," the old man takes its first half to refer to a male soul that has returned to God upon the body's death after living a solitary, childless life. Since procreation is a cardinal commandment of the Bible, this soul must "go forth" again in another body to take a wife and father the children it has failed to have.

This presumes, of course, that the "slave," in neglect of his religious obligations, was a bachelor. Yet what if he had a wife and the two tried to have children and did not succeed? In that case, the Bible says, his wife "shall go forth with him." God, who "does not stint on the wages of any of His creatures," the old man of Mishpatim tells us, will cause her soul to return to earth with her husband's, so that "they can be reborn together and joined together as before." The two souls will find each other in their new incarnation and have the offspring they were unable to have the first time.

So far, so good. Now, however, comes another verse in Mishpatim, which explains the procedure to be followed if the slave refuses to leave his master: "And if the slave shall plainly say, 'I love my master, my wife, and my children; I will not go forth free,' then his master shall bring him unto the judges . . . and his master shall bore his ear through with an awl, and he shall serve him forever." Fair enough—but wait a minute. "*And my children*?" Hasn't the old man just said that this soul is childless? "Old man, old man!" he chides himself, only now realizing, or pretending to realize (for perhaps he has reverted to playing the simple donkey driver), the contradiction. "The text tears down the building you have built!"

Exhorting himself to greater effort as if his mind were the donkey he was driving, the old man now strives to rescue his parable. Even if the couple has had children, he explains, the husband's soul may be guilty of other sins of which his wife's soul is innocent, so that it must atone for them by itself in a new *gilgul*. Yet suppose this soul not only loves God and desires to remain in His presence, it also loves its wife and children and does not want to start a new family with another woman, as it must do if it returns to earth. God, the old man assures us, will reward it for its faithfulness:

> What does God do? Though He was going to make [the husband's soul] return in another incarnation, so that it might make restitution in this world for what it has done [in a previous life], He does not force it to do so. He brings it before the tribunal of heaven [the judges of the biblical text], which sentences it to punishment [the text's painful awl] . . . and no other penance is required.

The husband's soul, which prefers to be punished in Gehenna rather than return to earth and be disloyal to its wife and children, is granted its wish. On the day of the resurrection, all will be restored to each other in their original bodies. Unlike the woman of the Sadducees' question to Jesus, neither husband nor wife will have to debate whom to choose, having been wed to each other alone. The homily of the old man of Mishpatim turns out to be as much about love—love between a man and a woman, love in a family, God's love of such love—as it is about reincarnation.

❧

In the centuries following the Zohar's composition, kabbalistic circles came to consider reincarnation a near universal fate. The souls of sinners were now thought to require, as a matter of course, not only the purgation of Gehenna, but a corrective experience such as mere punishment could not provide. Called *tikkun* or "repair," this experience—part of the grander kabbalistic undertaking of "repairing" the spiritual fractures in creation—involved the soul's atoning, by acts of awareness, reparation, and completion, for misdeeds or omissions in a previous life.

The idea of *tikkun* gained particularly wide currency with the advent of the Lurianic school of kabbalah in Palestine in the sixteenth century, in the hilltop town of Safed in the Galilee, from where it spread rapidly throughout the Jewish world. The figure for which it was named, Rabbi Yitzhak Luria Ashkenazi—more commonly known as the Ari or "Lion" of Safed—was said to be so adept a diagnostician of *tikkun* that he could tell from a glance at someone what repair his or her soul needed and why.

There are many stories about the Ari's powers, most appearing in a collection, *Shivhey ha-Ari* or "The Praises of the Lion," put together by a disciple. According to one, he was asked by a pupil for permission to travel abroad. While offering no objection, Luria told the young man that if he set out, he would meet and marry a beautiful woman who would die after six months and bequeath him a certain sum of money. The pupil went abroad and Luria's prediction came true. When he returned home brokenhearted, the Ari explained to him that the woman's soul had formerly inhabited the body of a man who had befriended him in a previous life and then behaved badly toward him for a period of half a year, causing him financial loss. Now this soul had made restitution by returning the exact sum lost after first providing six months of happiness to offset the six months of sorrow.

Another story about Luria is more complex. A fellow inhabitant of Safed was Moshe Alsheikh, a leading rabbinic scholar and author of legal commentaries. Once, it is related, Alsheikh asked the Ari why he had never been invited to join the latter's inner mystical circle. The answer given him was that he, Alsheikh ,was a "spark" of the soul of the Mishnaic sage Hutzpit the Interpreter, the Greek and Latin translator of Gamaliel I, and that, having mastered all of Judaism's esoteric secrets in his prior incarnation, he had no need to occupy himself with them now; rather, his task was to perfect his knowledge of rabbinic law. The Ari then proposed a curious test. On the eve of the Sabbath, he said, Alsheikh should sit in a place by which he and his disciples would pass on their way to welcome the Sabbath Queen in the hills outside Safed. If Alsheikh saw them, he would know he had been put off with a lame excuse. If he didn't, it would prove that he had been told the truth. Alsheikh dressed in his Sabbath clothes, went to sit in the appointed place, fell into a deep sleep, and failed to see the entourage go by.

Of course, since we owe this story to a disciple of Luria's, it might have been invented to conceal the fact that

Alsheikh was simply not interested in Luria's teachings—one of which was that souls emitted "sparks" that could transmigrate to many bodies at once, just as a single candle can light many wicks. Although probably deriving from the need to explain how the different bodies inhabited by the same reincarnated soul could all share it in the resurrection, the doctrine of sparks took on a life of its own in the Ari's thought, which postulated intricate relationships of spark families. Alsheikh was not the only incarnation of Hutzpit in his generation. Others were, too. Nor, though they shared certain traits and affinities, would all have been charged with the same *tikkun*. Hutzpit was indeed known more as linguist and preacher than as a legal scholar, but not every spark of his soul would be expected, like Alsheikh's, to compensate for this by exhaustively mastering rabbinic law.

The ramifications did not stop there. Medieval Jewish philosophy, following in the wake of Islamic and Greek thought, divided the soul into three faculties: the *nefesh* or vital soul, which was responsible for basic biological functions; the *ru'ah* or passional soul, which was the seat of the emotions; and the *neshamah* or intellectual soul, which endowed humankind with its mental and spiritual faculties. This tripartite division was adopted by kabbalistic thought, too—and in Lurianic kabbalah, each faculty was assumed able to transmigrate on its own, so that someone's *nefesh* might be reincarnated in one person, his *ru'ah* in another, and his *neshamah* in a third. Hutzpit the Interpreter's *nefesh*, for example, was said by Luria to have descended from Adam's son Cain via Samuel, Elijah, and others; having then "sparked," it was also found in Hutzpit's contemporary Akiva, who was put to death together with Hutzpit as one of the "ten martyrs of the empire" executed by the Romans in the second century. Yet at the same time, Hutzpit's *neshamah* came from Abel, Cain's murdered brother, and had also been in Moses and Judah the Prince.

Lurianic kabbalah, as the great historian of Jewish mysticism Gershom Scholem put it, "placed the Jew in an ineluctable entanglement of transmigrations." The soul you were born with could be the product of any number of souls, parts of souls, and sparks of souls joined together; when you died, they departed your body like a group of travelers who, having banded together for a while, now head in different directions. Your physical constitution might be reincarnated in one person, your emotional makeup in another, your psyche in a third. If all souls came from the primordial spiritual body of Adam, as the Lurianists believed, then human history was a process of their being shuffled and reshuffled like a pack of cards until, when the grand cycle was completed, the deck would be restored to its original state and every soul, its faculties purged, perfected, and reunited, would revert to its rightful place.

In the reincarnations of the Lurianists, you did not live on as a distinct person any more than you did in the immortality of the philosophers. Fragments of souls roamed the universe, sometimes recognizing themselves in other fragments, sometimes joined by them. Known as *sod ha-ibbur* or "the mystery of impregnation," such joinings could happen for good or for bad. A weaker soul might be temporarily "impregnated" with a stronger soul wishing to come to its aid in a crisis or in the performance of a difficult task. It might be cleaved to by a dybbuk, a homeless soul looking for a habitation. At one end of its spectrum, Lurianic

Kabbalah was abstrusely complicated, demanding years of study to be thoroughly comprehended. At its other end, it merged with popular superstitions about ghosts, demons, haunts, and hostile and friendly spirits such as were common in every premodern culture.

Strange things might happen to a soul. Sa'adia would have been shocked by some of them. The Safed businessman Ya'akov Abulafia was returning home from a trip to Egypt when he lost his way and wandered for hours in the desert before spying a man plowing with a team of oxen. Heading in his direction, Abulafia saw that the man was whipping the beasts mercilessly—yet all of a sudden he became an ox himself while the oxen became men and began to whip him. They took turns in this manner until sunset, when all three reassumed human form. Upon learning that Abulafia came from Safed, they begged him to ask the Ari to release them from their ordeal. Luria complied, telling Abulafia that the three were being punished for having shaven off their earlocks in their former lives. This was appropriate retribution, he explained, because the Hebrew word *par*, "bull," has the same initial letters as does *pe'at roshkhem*, "the corners of your heads," which biblical law forbids trimming.

Another time, in the middle of teaching a lesson, Luria asked for a mousetrap. His puzzled disciples brought one and set it, and at once a rat was caught. "What did you think?" Luria berated it. "That no one, God forbid, would judge you for informing on your fellow Jews and ruining them?" The rat burst out crying and pleaded for its soul to be released from its rat's body and sent to Gehenna, but Luria refused. "You're not worthy of hell," he told it, ordering his disciples to open the trap. "Be gone!"

❧

Rats are the one animal I loathe. They get into the attic next to my study by climbing trees and crawling under the eaves of the roof, and they run around there and make a racket, sometimes erupting in a frenzy as if playing tag along the roof beams. It's worse when one escapes into the house. I've killed dozens of them—poisoned them, trapped and drowned them, bludgeoned them to death, once dispatched one in the kitchen sink. The poisoned ones go off to die in some dark corner, swelling and stinking until they pop open with a foul burst. The drowned ones I carry by the long strings of their tails and fling into bushes far from the house. The black beads of their eyes bulge as though still struggling to breathe under water.

I too think I might prefer hell to being a rat, even if hell were as horrid a place as the Middle Ages pictured it. Its torments far surpassed those of the hell of early Christianity, for the medieval world had a morbid preoccupation with sin and its punishment. One reason it did was that, as Christianity and Islam evolved into ruling religions with vast domains populated by their adherents, hell became a destination less for infidels than for the millions of believers who failed to live by their professed beliefs: the weak-willed, the deceivers, the fraudulent espousers of the faith. "The hypocrites are surely in the lowest depths of the fire," says the Koran about Jahannam, the Muslim Gehenna, and paying lip service to the truth while flouting it is clearly a more heinous offense than failing to recognize it in the first place. If Dante's *Inferno*, the most celebrated description of hell in world literature, concentrates disproportionately on its author's fellow Italian Catholics,

this is not just because Dante was using the poem to settle
scores with people he knew or had firsthand knowledge of.
It is also because Italy, as the home of the papacy, was medieval Christianity's citadel, and no sin is greater than that
of the guardian of the citadel who betrays it.

This is why the *Inferno* ends at the bottom of hell's ninth
and nethermost circle with five traitors: the Pisan noble-
man Ugolino della Gherardesca, who deserted the Guelphs,
Dante's political party, for its rivals, the Ghibellines, and
ate his children in prison to keep from starving; Dante's
contemporary Fra Alberigo, a friar who murdered his kins-
men while they were guests in his home; Judas Iscariot,
who informed on Jesus to the Romans; and the assassins
of Caesar, his friends Brutus and Cassius. Dante gives each
his fitting deserts. Ugolino is condemned to chew on the
head of his equally duplicitous jailor, the Pisan archbishop
Ruggiero degli Ubaldino, with unsated hunger. Alberigo is
frozen in ice that cakes his eyes, forcing his penitent tears
excruciatingly back into them. Judas, Brutus, and Cassius
are themselves chewed on by the arch-traitor Satan, their
heads in his mouth and their legs flailing in agony.

Judaism, while remaining the faith of a small minority, was part of its environment and did not escape
being influenced by the grimness of the medieval imagination. The medieval *Masekhet Gehinnom*, "The Tractate
of Gehenna," an account of a visit to hell by our intrepid
traveler Yehoshua ben Levi, reports his seeing there men
and women hung from their feet, hands, noses, tongues,
and breasts, forced to swallow hot coals and eat their own
flesh, and hurled from fire into snow and back again. Each
punishment, we are told, has its own special angel to ad-
minister it. "One comes, exacts retribution, and goes his

way, and then a second and a third. . . . To what might it be compared? To a debtor with many creditors who is brought before the king. 'What can I do?' the king tells them. 'Take him and divide what he has among you.' And so the soul in hell is put in the charge of cruel angels who divide it among them."

Pietistic tales going back to medieval and early post-medieval times bear witness to the fear of frightful punishment after death with which many Jews lived. In his *Sefer ha-Hasidim* or "Book of the Pious," Yehuda he-Hasid, a prominent rabbi in the German towns of Speyer and Regensburg in the late twelfth and thirteenth centuries, writes of a Jew condemned to hell for nothing worse than thinking of his own enjoyment rather than of God's bounty when blessing the food that he ate. The tiniest infraction, such as failing to say "Amen" after a single blessing, could have extreme consequences.

Sins of omission are also the theme of a story about the seventeenth-century rabbi Yitzhak Hayyot. In a near-death vision of the next world while on his sickbed, Hayyot saw a woman and her son bound to each other and dragged behind a carriage driven by devils, their hands cuffed and their feet in chains, while their tormentors flayed their skin and proclaimed, "Thus shall be done to the woman whom God blessed with a Torah scholar for a husband but who did not raise her son as one." Each time mother and son passed out from pain they were revived and flogged again, until the scholar, hearing their screams from his place in paradise, descended to rescue them.

Following the family, Hayyot arrived at the gates of paradise just as a saintly Jew who had recently died was brought there for trial by the heavenly tribunal. Legions of

angels dressed in white came to testify to his moral recti-
tude and punctilious ritual observance. When they were
done, the head of the court posed a last question: had the
man taken care to obey the injunction of the *Shulhan Arukh,*
the authoritative codification of Jewish law, to channel his
mind to thoughts of God's greatness whenever uttering
His name? The defendant's knees shook as more angels,
this time dressed in black, gave evidence of the numerous
times he had failed to do this. The judges tore their robes
as though in mourning and the chief justice exclaimed:
"You miserable drop [of human sperm]! Because you took
no heed, you must either return again to earth or descend
to the terrible furnace of Gehenna."

The choice was worth weighing because, while the medieval Gehenna was ghastlier than the Talmudic one, the
two shared the same saving feature: a Jew's term in them
lasted only twelve months. Moreover, whereas the Talmud
decrees that the souls of the worst sinners are then incinerated, the Tractate of Gehenna is more clement. All of
the damned, it declares, will be restored to life from their
ashes, their faces "black as the rim of a pot"; will proclaim
to God, "Fairly hast Thou judged us, fairly hast thou sentenced us"; and will be admitted to paradise. Even Gentiles
will be released after serving a full year in each of hell's
seven circles of fire, in every one of which are 60,000
houses with 6,000 scribes in every house keeping records
with pens dipped in inkpots of gall.

In the Middle Ages, too, the God of Israel was more merciful than the God of the Christians, who turned His back
on the eternal suffering of the damned. Reincarnation was
less painful but could continue cycle after cycle and assume repellent forms. Hell meant taking one's medicine

and getting it over with. Its sufferings short-lived, it was the sinner's shortcut to heaven.

One person not in need of shortcuts was the author of the *Shulhan Arukh*, Yosef Karo. The recognized leader of Safed's Jewish community in the years before Isaac Luria settled there, Karo was in his lifetime guaranteed a place in paradise by his *maggid*. It was an age in which *maggidim*, celestial informants who cultivated relationships with deserving individuals on earth and revealed heavenly secrets to them, were believed to be in communication with more than one rabbi. Yet Karo's *maggid* was special, being no less, so he was convinced, than a personification of the Mishnah. A stern ascetic who regularly chastised himself for the sinful pleasure he took in ordinary activities like eating and drinking, Karo was reassured by his *maggid* that he would, despite these lapses of conduct, enter heaven after his death in great glory. "All the saints of paradise," he was told, "will go forth to meet you and greet you with songs of praise [and] will lead you before them like a bridegroom to the wedding canopy."

There would be, his *maggid* informed Karo, fourteen canopies, under each of which he would be clothed with another heavenly garment before being seated on a gold throne to discuss the Torah with his peers. After six months of such study, there would be a gala seven-day "banquet of the Law" with him as its sole speaker and teacher. "Pay homage to the holy son of the King on High!" the saints would proclaim in his honor. "Pay homage to the likeness of the king!" He would then be led to thirteen "rivers of balsam," immersing himself in each while removing one of his garments. The last of these would be shed in a river of fire, after which he would be clothed in a pure white robe and ushered by the archangel Michael into the presence of the Holy One Blessed Be He. From this point on, Karo's *maggid* told him, "I have no more permission to reveal anything, 'For neither has the eye seen what He has prepared for those who wait for Him.'"

Whether the "banquet of the Law" included gustatory or merely spiritual nourishment is moot. Inherited from the Talmudic period, heaven's ambiguous nature continued to tease in medieval times, with serious rabbinic discourse tending to a less and popular religion to a more literal interpretation of the next world's promised delights. Like other rabbinic versions of paradise, Karo's draws on earlier sources. Its river of fire can be traced all the way back to Enoch I; its canopies, perfumed waters, and sessions of Torah study to the vision of Yehoshua ben Levi; its concluding verse from Isaiah to Yohanan bar Nafha's advisement against trying to imagine the world-to-come. Tardily heeding Yohanan's counsel, Karo's *maggid* now falls silent, for the presence of God is ineffable.

Karo's *maggid* also explained to him the reason for the House of Hillel and the House of Shammai's disagreement about the unlived life. It did so in commenting on the tradition that the second-century Rabbi Meir owned a Torah scroll in which the words *tov me'od*, "very good," in Genesis 1:31 ("And God looked up all that He had created and behold, it was very good") were written as *tov mot*, "it is good to die." This, the *maggid* said, was in keeping with the House of Shammai's opinion. Since the soul that dwells with God before its earthly descent returns to Him after death if it has lived righteously, life exposes it to the risk of sin and to temporary or permanent exile from heaven while offering it nothing in the way of reward that it didn't have to begin with. It would be preferable not to live at all.

Why, then, did the House of Hillel think it better to be born? Because, said the *maggid*, the unborn soul has a need to prove its worth. It is like a charitable ward in a palace who, "ashamed to eat the unearned bread of the king . . . longs to come into this world and engage in [the study of] Torah and [the observance of] the commandments so that it may eat the king's bread without shame." Life is a perilous adventure in which the soul is given the chance to find its way back to its divine source by its own efforts. Had it never lived and died, it would have indeed remained safely and uninterruptedly in God's presence, but with the awareness of being there on sufferance. Now, it can be confident that it is there by right.

The third great innovative departure of the Jewish Middle Ages was "secular" Hebrew literature. (The quotation marks are called for because "secular" in medieval times meant a relative freedom from religious norms and restrictions, not the strict separation from religion, or even opposition to it, that the word implies today.) Dealing with numerous subjects that were beyond the ken of traditional religious writing, or in styles unacceptable to it, this literature even had its own Dante, his contemporary Immanuel of Rome. Immanuel was a biblical commentator, one of the earliest practitioners of the Petrarchan sonnet, and the last Hebrew master of the Arabic genre known as *maqama*, a form of rhymed, narrative prose that commonly featured a roguish hero and his picaresque adventures. The twenty-eight long chapters of Immanuel's "Notebooks," as they are called, recount a series of such episodes, such as the time the rogue's wealthy patron challenges him to break down the defenses of a beautiful but haughtily virginal young lady with his amorous poetry, or the time he prescribes for a patient, while posturing as a physician, a poultice of wolf's horns, chicken milk, marble juice, and moonlight, and has to flee for his life. The first of these tales ends on an uncharacteristically somber note when, wooed by her seducer's poems, the young lady falls in love with him, proposes a tryst, and pines away from shame and grief when she receives the cruelly rebuking answer that his love has been feigned.

The last chapter of the Notebooks is a grand coda to all this: a tour of heaven and hell obviously inspired by Dante's *Divine Comedy*. As Dante had the poet Virgil for his guide, so Immanuel has the prophet Daniel, who first takes him to Gehenna to view various scenes of torment. In a typical one, he beholds a sinner, "crowned with thorns of punishment, nose plugged with human excrement, soundly flogged and roundly whipped while from his sex, which was enclaspéd by an asp, a black bile dripped." The reprobate is then taken to a tower and "cast far down upon the rocks, torn apart by wolf and fox, pierced by arrows, lanced by darts, dipped in pitch and boiled in tar." Immanuel asks, "Who is this man?" and is told by Daniel that while on earth he was a dissolute Torah scholar who gave free rein to his sexual passions with every consenting "Moabite and Ammonite, Jewess, Christian, and Egyptian" he could lay hands on.

Immanuel spends less time in heaven. While there, he spies many of the great figures of Jewish tradition; meets David, Isaiah, Ezekiel, Moses, Solomon, and other biblical authors and is praised by them for his commentaries on their books; sees his patrons, the wealthy Italian Jews who have supported him, and is shown,

> its footstool scintillant with light, a throne that shone with tint so bright that I longed to sit in it. "O say, I pray," I begged my guide, "for whom have this wondrous chair and jeweled stool been set aside?" And he replied: "The chair, I swear, is Judah's, Joseph's lionhearted brother, preeminent among the other sons of Jacob, and the stool with its bijou will be sat upon by you, his very secretary."

As skillful as such light semi-verse is, Dante it isn't. Nor was Immanuel like Yosef Karo, who solemnly believed his *maggid*'s promises. (Karo actually issued a rabbinical ban on the Notebooks' first printed edition.) Immanuel's heaven and hell are spoofs not only of Dante but of the conventional Jewish notions of his time—which, while he put them to literary use to denounce vice and false piety and laud his own achievements, he clearly took none too seriously. How, after all, can anyone be flung from a tower, dismembered by wild animals, and then shot, stabbed, and boiled in tar? Dante, too, of course, did not necessarily think that hell was really as he described it, but his descriptions have the passion, moral seriousness, and imaginative exactness of high art. Immanuel's never rise above the wanly generic. He himself, he writes elsewhere in the Notebooks, was an admirer of Maimonides, called by him "a beacon for all who seek in darkness," and presumably he shared the latter's view of the afterlife.

The heaven and hell of the Notebooks are not overt parody. They never cross the line between entertainment and open mockery. But to write merely entertainingly about what is dreadful or awesome to others is a form of mockery, too. It tells us that even in the deep Middle Ages there were educated, Hebrew-reading Jews (Immanuel was a popular author in his day) who, while loyal to their religion, were not offended when the afterlife was written about tongue-in-cheek. Some may have been influenced, like Immanuel, by Maimonides and the philosophers. (Nahmanides, for example, thought that while hell was a real place, its punishment was simply the sinful soul's extinction, the soul being a subtle form of the element of fire, by whose chthonian presence in the earth it was absorbed after death instead of ascending on high.) Others may have retained the old biblical sense of death's finality, which never vanished from Judaism entirely. The medieval Christianity that produced Dante's *Inferno* could not have produced the last chapter of Immanuel's Notebooks because Christianity first sprouted in the soil of a fervent belief in personal immortality, without which it was hardly imaginable. Judaism's roots went deeper. It could shed that belief while still remaining itself.

Immanuel of Rome is not one of the great medieval Hebrew poets. Shmuel Hanagid is the greatest of them all. I say this advisedly, having lived intimately with his poetry for over ten years. That's how long it took me to translate the sixty-four poems in a "verse autobiography" of him that I published under the title *Grand Things to Write a Poem On*.

Hanagid—the Hebrew epithet means "the governor"—is one of Jewish history's most extraordinary figures. Not since the time of Judah the Prince had any Jew wielded the power that he did. Born in 993 in Cordoba, in Muslim Andalusia, he settled as a young man in Granada and swiftly rose to prominence at its royal court. For over two decades he served as the grand vizier of Granada's kingdom, which contended with Seville for supremacy in the south of Spain, and as a military commander in its battles. He also found time to be a leading rabbinic scholar, a lover of wine and good company, an inveterate philanderer, a deeply religious personality, a devoted father to the son who succeeded him after his death, a ruthless enemy to his foes, and a prolific poet whose verse reflected these many sides of him.

In 1041, when Hanagid was forty-eight, his older brother Yitzhak, a prominent Jewish communal figure in his own right, died after a brief illness. Though having lived in different places, the two men were extremely close. During the following year, Hanagid wrote a sequence of nineteen poems about Yitzhak's death. Briefly annotated by his son Yehosef, they are, apart from their lyrical beauty, an unparalleled document of mourning.

The first of these poems, written, Yehosef tells us, when Yitzhak was in critical condition, is a prayer for his recovery. In it we already encounter the deep sense of guilt that runs through the entire sequence. Hanagid had lived a life of political intrigue, bloody warfare, and voluptuary pleasures; it was he, he felt, who deserved to be punished, not Yitzhak. "If harsh, Lord, you must be," the poem's last lines read,

> be so with me
> And with my miscreant ways, and let my brother be.
> I am the sinner. Why take him?
> Visit on me Your justice. I will be in.

But Yitzhak dies and Hanagid learns of it in the next poem, as he is on his way to his brother with his own physician. His first, instinctive reaction is denial. "Be still and may dust fill your mouth!" he berates the bearer of the tidings.

> Would every woe were your woe!
> Might they bury you who bore you!
> The doctor with me many like him healed and has made
>   well,
> And you say he is dead who led his age and people?
> I tell you, he but sleeps!

By Poem 4, in which Hanagid rends his garments, his heart "in tatters more than any rag, more shattered than the dishes you will smash," the reality of his brother's death has set in. And in Poem 5, so has its permanence:

> Give up, my soul, all thought of seeing him again.
> Learn to live without him—and if you
> Find that unthinkable, die too!

The sixth poem describes the funeral, before which Hanagid performs the ritual cleansing and shrouding of his brother's body. Afterward, those in attendance offer words of comfort. His anger at their trite assurances that he will get over what he is sure he never will erupts bitterly.

> Aye, when I had washed him,
> And dressed him,

And laid him out on his bier
And walked him on his last way,
And stepped forth from my circle of friends to lower
   him into the grave ,
And they said,
"He has taken him to His place,"
Did I not, stricken, say,
"Would He had taken me in his place"?
And when they said,
"Time heals all wounds,"
I answered them:
"A curse on time and its cure!
Lord, You can have back this life,
Which, my brother dead,
Is too much to endure!"

The day after the funeral, Hanagid returns to the cemetery. Standing by the fresh earth on his brother's grave, he
speaks to him. Yet far from making him feel that Yitzhak,
though dead, is still approachable, the nearness of the
grave fills him with horror at the thought of the physical
dissolution already taking place in it.

    Are you all right?
              Shall I speak louder?
And will you hear me if I raise a voice
That's cracked with grief?
Why don't you answer me?
Say how you passed the night in your new home!
Did you begin to feel your skin peel from your bones,
Your jaw unsocketed?
Did life's last sap run slowly out of you
As my tears trickle from me, one by one?

The eighth poem is set during the seven-day period of the shiva, which Hanagid spends in his brother's residence. Again he angrily refuses solace. His resentment of the condolence callers' invocation of time's curative powers is now compounded by his annoyance at their well-intended cliché that everyone goes through the same experience. What do they know about *his* experience? How can anyone but himself understand what his brother was to him? "Ah, you would comfort me, would you?" he asks.

> As if any comfort there could be,
> Or any life
> Or sanity,
> After putting Yitzhak in the grave!
> Stand back, then,
> Save your breath—
> Or better yet,
> Find me a fitter friend,
> Such as a jackal that has lost its young,
> And let it howl, and me weep, and see
> Which one of us will be grief's champion.
> My friends,
> Don't think that you have known loss like mine,
> Or that my Yitzhak's death is like all men's.

The shiva ends. Rather than feeling relief at being left at last with his own emotions, however, Hanagid must now confront the reality that the world, having done its religious duty, has moved on past his brother's death, while he is just starting to live it. "Over now," he declares in the ninth poem, "are mourning's days, / but over not each morning's daze, / the days of pain, / the stomach-churning nights." The real ordeal is still ahead of him. As much as he chafed under death's distracting ceremonies, they helped get him through the first week. Now he is on his own.

The days go by. The initial month of mourning draws to a close—and with it Hanagid's old ways and habits, stunned into abeyance by his brother's death, begin to stir again. Although his heart, he assures Yitzhak in Poem 10, remains "split in two, / half consumed in ashes / and half lived in by you," so that "in half your constant image I behold, / in half my anguish smolders uncontrolled," life reasserts itself. Grief is now joined by dismay that grief is weakening. This precipitates a new crisis in Poem 11:

> What,
> My brother scarcely dead a month,
>   And I already long for bathhouses, amusements,
>   dalliance?
> Can I so faithless be, a traitor to my cause?
> Let me mourn on, then: days desolate, hands struck in
>   grief, beard unbarbered, meals chewed in solitude,
>   all consolation spurned,
> Bereft.
> He lies untongued. What voice to weep with except mine
>   does he have left?

But even as he fights normality's return, Hanagid is forced to admit that the comforters he disdained have spoken truly: time *does* heal, however slowly, however one resists the healing. When the first month ends, he goes again to visit Yitzhak's grave. "He traveled," Yehosef writes in a

note to Poem 12, "until he had nearly reached the cemetery,
when he stopped and thought":

Suppose the ocean lay between us,
Don't you think I still would leave
Everything to come and see you
And run the last steps to your grave,
Since not to do so would be treason
To our bond of brother love?

O my brother!
Soon I will sit by your grave,
And the hurt in my heart will be like the hurt
when you died.
For if I say hello to you,
You will not answer me;
Nor will you come to greet me
When I come to your country;
Nor will you laugh, nor will I laugh
At any pleasantry;
Nor will you see my face again,
Nor will I ever see
Yours either,
Now that you have made the earth your hostelry.

Adieu and fare you well,
My father's eldest and my mother's son,
And may God's spirit rest upon your soul.
I shall return to my own soil, and you shall rest in
yours,
And I shall sleep and wake anon, and you shall wake no
more,
And may the flame of parting burn till I too cross
Death's door!

The "treason" Hanagid fears committing is inevitable. Though kept alive by him, the "flame of parting" will be a modest one, not the raging conflagration of Poem 10. And the fifteenth poem marks another turning point. In it, Hanagid attends a shiva himself, one whose family has lost a beloved brother, too. He has now crossed the divide between mourners and comforters to its other side, even though he seeks to assure Yitzhak that "every tear those mourners cried / fell, in my heart, for you." Yes, his experience has been his own and no one else's—but so is the experience of the family he is visiting. Ultimately, we all *do* go through the same thing.

Poem 18 is written on the anniversary of Yitzhak's death. For the first time in the sequence there is humor, a wry wistfulness testifying how far Hanagid has come from his initial devastation. He can now smile at the fantasy of seeing Yitzhak again and speak to him, not in the distraught and guilty tones of the earlier poems, but with a bantering camaraderie:

> Twelve months gone by, and still the huntsman Death
> Holds you ensnared! Or do you like his clay so well,
> Find worms such better company than men,
> That you would stay?
>   Just think, my dear,
> If you could shake the dust off, drop in on your old haunts,
>   chat with old friends again, and let me
>   tell you of my latest conquests!
> If only a man—flesh putrefied, bones dry as twigs,
>   a prisoner (soul heaven-prised) of earth, a meal
>   for maggots, a banquet of stuffed shrouds—could
>   do it!

All this leads up to the magnificent nineteenth and final
poem, written, according to Yehosef, when at last Hanagid's
grief had passed and, "consoled, he mourned no more." It is
a hymn of thanksgiving and acceptance—of thanksgiving
for being able to accept his acceptance, both of Yitzhak's
death and of his own recovery from it:

Praise be to God who hears all prayers
   and whom all men should praise;
Who grants mankind His kindness as the sun
Bestows on all its all-beholden rays;
Who makes all things hard, gross, recalcitrant,
Seem yielding and inviting at the start
(Like blades of grass; like occupations, trades;
   like everything newborn, though it as tangled
   as an oak tree grows to be)
Except for melancholy,
Which lusty comes into this world and fades;
For if it did not lighten in men's hearts,
No heart could keep from breaking from its weight.

No tongue can count or words recount God's grace to
   men!
For I,
Who in my grief declared that of despair my soul would
   die
Before it reached the end of sorrow's hemmed-in way,
Now walk abroad in comfort,
My sorrow sloughed away
As my poor brother's flesh is in the grave.
And though compassion in my bowels still does stir
Until I groan like many men possessed,
Most times I am like one who in his heart

Unburdened is of troubles laid to rest.
Thus, the Lord sickens and strikes down,
And heals and quickens him whom He has stricken.

May He who shrouds Himself in nebulae
And to the earth my brother's shrouds consigned
Forgive him every sin
And mercifully his virtue keep in mind.
And may the merits of his fathers stand him in good
    stead
As his will stand me now that he is dead!

It has taken Hanagid a year to reach some kind of clo-
sure. His poems' division of this year into the news of his
brother's death, the funeral, the first week, the first month,
and the following eleven months closely follows the peri-
odization of the tractate of Semahot and Jewish ritual. Is
this only because he was mourning as a Jew, or does the
Jewish calendar of mourning reflect the natural workings
of the human heart? A week, more or less, may be what is
needed to absorb death's first shock; a month for the numb-
ness to start wearing off; a year to feel fully oneself again.
The cycle of the year, at the end of which nature has returned to its starting point while human life has not, is
emblematic of all that will never and will always change,
of all that will always and will never pass. Although not
the only imaginable amount of time in which to mourn, it
seems a right one.

Many of the bereavement customs referred to in
Hanagid's poems are still practiced by Jews today. Others,
though mentioned in Semahot, no longer are, such as the
smashing of dishes or the return to the cemetery on the
morrow of the funeral. A fresh grave, Semahot instructs

us, should be visited daily for the first three days after burial to make sure its occupant has not been mistakenly interred in a state of catalepsy and is now calling out. In one case known to the Mishnah of a man buried alive and rescued, he lived for an additional twenty-five years. In another, a father of sons fathered five more before being buried for a second and last time.

Dishes were still being hurled into graves at Jewish funerals one-hundred-fifty years after Hanagid's time: we know this from Maimonides, whose Mishneh Torah, the first encyclopedic compendium of rabbinic law since the Mishnah, includes a section on *hilkhot avel,* "the laws of the mourner." Mourners, Maimonides writes there, "should be educated not to be destructive by laying waste to household vessels or smashing them. It is better to give them to the poor than to fling them to the worms and maggots."

Maimonides was against waste in general. (Wasted time, especially: the Mishneh Torah was written to free Jewish minds for the study of philosophy by eliminating the need to collate, compare, and rank the different rulings of innumerable rabbis.) In commenting on Semahot's permission to hold a wedding ceremony during the shiva, he raises the question whether the customary wedding banquet can be held, too. His answer: if the meat has already been butchered before death occurred and cannot be resold, so that it will spoil unless cooked and eaten, the banquet may take place. If it hasn't been, or if a buyer can be found for it, the banquet should be postponed.

Maimonides does not generally cite his sources or bother to justify his concisely worded rulings, which he expects will be accepted on the basis of his authority alone. In this he differs from Nahmanides, who also wrote a treatise on death and mourning. Called *Torat ha-Adam*, "The Manner of Man," from a verse in the book of Samuel, it is, alongside Maimonides' summation, one of the two most consulted medieval manuals on the subject. Nahmanides' method in it is to review the gamut of opinion on a given matter before presenting and explaining, sometimes lengthily, his own.

On the question of a wedding feast during the shiva, he disagrees with Maimonides. One difference between mourners and the family of a bride or groom, he points out, is that the former have food prepared for them and their condolence callers by friends and neighbors while the latter must feed their guests at their own expense. The crucial question, therefore, is not waste, but wealth or poverty. If the mourners are well-off and can afford to buy quantities of meat a second time, the wedding banquet should be rescheduled even if the meat will spoil; if not, the banquet should take place.

Such deliberations have a fussy practicality that may seem absurd in the face of death's immensity. *My clothing can be stitched and laundered white*, Shmuel Hanagid exclaims, *but my torn heart can never be repaired!* Yet precisely this is the point: the mourner's heart *must* be repaired. Death is a ruthless enemy that will eventually cut him down, too—a sobering thought that is part of death's shock. ("Throughout the first three days" of mourning, Maimonides writes, "let the mourner imagine the sword [of the Angel of Death] resting on his own throat; from the third day to the seventh, stowed in the corner [of his room]; from then on, passing close to him in the street.") All the more reason, then, not to let mourners be carried away. Society has a responsibility to prevent this from happening.

Maimonides would have disapproved of Shmuel Hanagid's emotionalism. Not to mourn for the dead at all, he says, would be "cruel." Still, one must mourn in moderation. "A person should not go to too great lengths over his dead," he states, "for it says [in the book of Jeremiah], 'Weep ye not for the dead, nor bemoan them'—that is, [weep] no more than is the way of the world. Whoever exceeds the way of the world is being foolish."

In the summer of 1042, during or soon after the year of mourning for his brother, Shmuel Hanagid found himself with the Granadan army near the besieged city of Granada's ally Lorca. About to go into battle against the besiegers, the Granadans were outnumbered and fighting far from home, and the night before their planned attack Hanagid wrote this verse letter to his son:

Yehosef:
All that I have been through,
And all the peril I have taken on myself,
Have been for you—
And were it not for you, I long ago
Would have become a wanderer in this world
As have become so many in your time.
I write you the plain truth

(Who is there to write it but a father?)
And as I write death japes at us,
Its long mouth wide agape, and I know not
Whether in the morn, when the foe rises,
The battle will go for us or against us.
But if it happens to be fated, son, that never
Will I see you or you see me again,
Then when thou sittest and when thou risest
Mark my words.
May they be first to rouse you from your slumber,
And on the day there is no one to teach you,
Let them be your teachers and your guides.

In all your ways—
With all your soul—
With all your might—
Fear your Maker and Creator.
Study to be wise and sensible,
For wisdom is the only praise you need,
And sensibleness the sole pedestal.
Obey your mother;
Speak gently to your uncle and your kin;
Respect your friends;
Be loving to all creatures;
See, before all goods, to your good name.

Yehosef:
Give to each man what he asks of you,
And if you have it not, have a soft answer.
Share in what there is with those who need it,
Although in sharing, think of your need, too.
Make something of yourself! Do not make do
With what I've done, for doing's all.

Excel, exceed your elders—and yet be not
Unaccepting of those younger than you.
Ah, how much more I still could say regarding virtue
That you may have to find out for yourself.
If God brings me home, I'll tell you of it—
O may He save you from all harm!

Although the eleventh-century rabbi Eleazer ben Yitzhak
of Worms is generally credited with being the author of the
earliest of the so-called "ethical wills" of Jewish tradition—
letters of advice and admonishment to one's children, often
written close to an actual or feared death, that originated
in the Middle Ages—Hanagid's poem most likely came
first. Possibly because of its verse form and the atypical
circumstances of its composition, it has never been placed
alongside such better-known examples of the genre as the
renowned Arabic-Hebrew translator Yehuda ibn Tibbon's
long and touchingly querulous letter to his son Shmuel,
who had failed to live up to his expectations (as it turned
out, the chastised son was to surpass his father at his own
profession), or the Ramban's pithily pious counsel to his son
Nahman, which is still read in religious circles. In the ethical will, the silenced voice of the dead is restored, but it does
not speak to the mourner. It addresses the post-mourner
who is fully back to the difficult business of living.

Years ago, grieved by musing about possibly dying before my two daughters were fully grown, I had an idea: I
would sit down and write each of them a letter for every
one of her future birthdays in which I would share my
thoughts with her about the age she had reached. Every
year she would receive a letter from her dead father and be
accompanied by me in this way.

I never thought of it as such, but these letters would have been a kind of ethical will. In the end, I didn't write a single one of them. Perhaps the task was beyond me, and perhaps it simply would have been too sad. Yet not only is writing a more lasting form of expression than speech, it can also be an easier one. Although my daughters grew up long ago, I've never to this day said most of what I've wanted to say to them before I die. If I'm ever to do it, it looks as if I'll still have to write it.

CHAPTER FOUR

SURPRISINGLY, IT MIGHT SEEM, NEITHER THE TRACTATE OF
Semahot, nor Shmuel Hanagid's poem sequence, nor
Maimonides' *Hilkhot Avel,* mentions the *kaddish yatom,* the
orphan's or mourner's kaddish whose recital, more than
any other ritual, is identified in most minds with Jewish
mourning. For many Jews, "saying kaddish" in the year
after a death is a test of mourning's seriousness. The more
steadily it is recited in the course of its prescribed regimen
of thrice in *shaharit,* the daily morning service, and once
in *minhah* and *ma'ariv,* the afternoon and evening services,
the greater one's devotion to the memory of the deceased
is assumed to be.

It's not an easy test to pass. Traditional Jewish law ordains that the kaddish—the word means "sanctification"—be said only in a *minyan,* a prayer quorum of ten
or more eligible male worshipers; reciting it in privacy,
at one's own convenience, does not discharge the obligation. Apart from the week of the shiva, therefore, during
which observant Jews make sure to convene daily *minyans*
in the mourner's home, saying the kaddish on a regular
basis means attending synagogue twice a day (*minhah* and

ma'ariv are usually held together, the former right before and the latter right after sunset), month after month. This calls for resolve.

Moreover, once the year of mourning is over, the kaddish continues to be recited annually on the anniversary or (to call it by the commonly used Yiddish word that literally means "year time") *yortsayt* of the death. Popular religion attaches supreme importance to all this. The firstborn son of a family in Yiddish-speaking Eastern Europe was referred to as its "kaddish," the guarantor that there would be someone to say the prayer for his parents when they died even if no more male children were born after him. Mourners unable or unwilling to attend synagogue regularly often hired stand-ins to say the kaddish in their place. Heroic attempts not to miss the prayer are the stuff of Jewish folklore. One of Sholem Aleichem's "Railroad Stories" relates how a passenger on a train strives to assemble a makeshift *minyan* so that he can say the kaddish on the *yortsayt* of his son. Nine Jews, including the narrator, agree to join; a tenth declines because, as he says, "I don't happen to believe in such things." How the mourner lures the tenth man into taking part in the *minyan* anyway, recites the kaddish with such feeling that "a stone," the narrator says, "couldn't help being moved," and then cleverly puts the crass freethinker to shame forms the story's conclusion.

Written in a mixture of Hebrew and Aramaic and structured as an exchange between the mourner and the congregation, the kaddish is truly a moving prayer. Its words, the congregation's in italics, are:

Magnified and sanctified be His great name.
Amen!

In this world created by Him as He willed, may His
kingdom be fulfilled by Him in your lives and your
days and the lives of the whole House of Israel,
speedily and soon, and say: amen.
>
> *Amen! Let His great name be*
> *blessed forever and ever!*

Let His great name be blessed forever and ever!
Blessed, and praised, and glorified, and uplifted, and
acclaimed, and adored, and extolled, and exalted be
His holy name, blessed be He,
>
> *blessed be He!*

beyond all blessing, song, praise and consolation that
are uttered in this world, and say: amen.
>
> *Amen!*

May there be great peace from heaven and life upon us
and all Israel, and say: amen.
>
> *Amen!*

May the maker of peace in His heights make peace for
us and all Israel, and say: amen.
>
> *Amen!*

Not even a sensitive translation can convey the kaddish's full power, which owes as much to its sound as to its
sense. Its opening proclamation of *yitgadal ve-yitkadash,*
"Magnified and sanctified be," picked up and amplified
by the incantatory "Blessed and praised" phrase of *yitba-
rakh ve-yishtabakh ve-yitpa'ar ve-yitromam ve-yitnasey ve-
yit'hadar ve-yit'aleh ve-yit'halal;* its rolling internal rhyme
of *kol birkhata, shirata, tushbehata ve-nehemata,* "all blessing, song, praise, and consolation"; its alliterative insis-
tence on *ve-imru amen,* "and say amen": all these give its
celebration of God's greatness a solemn, swelling majesty.

But what does any of it have to do with mourning? Apart from the single word "consolation," there is nothing in the kaddish that might indicate it is meant to be said in a context of bereavement. It hails God not as a healer of private grief but as the redeemer of His people; in some, principally Sephardi versions of it, "May His kingdom be fulfilled" is followed by "and may He bring His redemption and hasten the coming of His messiah," while added to the penultimate entreaty for "peace from heaven and life upon us" is a request for "plenty, healing, solace, liberation, rescue and deliverance, atonement and forgiveness, redemption and salvation." The mourner prays in the kaddish for the living, not for the dead.

And in fact, when it originated in Talmudic times the kaddish was not a prayer of mourning at all. Rather, it was a paean of praise recited to mark the end of a session of Torah study, its opening words paralleled by Jesus' "Lord's Prayer," which has the same ancient rabbinic background. (In its common English version, this begins: "Our father in heaven, hallowed be Your name, Your will be done, Your kingdom come.") Practically identical to what eventually came to be the mourner's kaddish, this early kaddish differed from it in one respect: a supplication for the welfare of "our rabbis, their students, the students of their students, and all who engage in [the study of] Torah." Although today, known as the *kaddish d'rabanan* or "rabbis' kaddish," it, too, is recited as part of the synagogue service, this was not the case in antiquity.

How did the rabbis' kaddish become the mourner's kaddish? The process was set in motion by beliefs first expressed in a number of texts, of which the oldest are found in the Gemara. In the tractate of Berakhot, there is a story about Rabbi Yosi, who is told by Elijah: "When the people of Israel enter their synagogues and study houses and respond, 'Let His great name be blessed,' the Holy One Blessed Be He nods and says: 'Happy is the king who is praised thus in His dwellings!'" In Sota, Rava is quoted as saying that in an age in which sacrifice in the Temple no longer exists to atone for sin, the world is maintained by the recital of "the 'Let His great name be blessed' of aggadah." The term *aggadah,* literally, "telling," designates a midrashic homily or sermon, at the end of which the rabbis' kaddish was recited. Both passages inform us that the proclamation of "Let His great name be blessed" was considered a supreme affirmation of faith in the God of Israel.

A third text, familiar from Chapter 2, is the story of Rabbi Akiva and the sinner released from hell when his son recites the words "Blessed be God the Blessed One forever and ever"—words similar to those in the rabbis' kaddish. And finally, a fourth text is linked to Akiva, too. Named "The Alphabet of Rabbi Akiva" and dating to about 700, it consists of a series of midrashim on the twenty-two Hebrew letters. In the midrash on the letter *zayin* is the passage:

> In time to come, the Holy One Blessed Be He will sit expounding the Torah in paradise, and all the righteous will sit before him, and the entire entourage of heaven will stand by. . . . And when it is the turn of aggadah, Zerubavel the son of She'altiel will rise to his feet and say, "Magnified and sanctified [be His great name]," and his voice will travel from one end of the world to the other,

and all the world's inhabitants will say, "Amen." Even the sinful Israelites and righteous Gentiles in Gehenna will say "Amen," and the sound will fill the world, so that God will ask, "What is this great sound that I hear?" "Master of the universe," the angels will tell him, "it is the sinners of Israel and the righteous of the Gentiles saying 'Amen' in Hell." At once God's compassion will be greatly stirred and He will say, "What shall I do for them? They have been condemned by their own worse selves." Then the Holy One Blessed Be He will take the keys to Gehenna and hand them to [the archangels] Michael and Gabriel in the presence of all the righteous, and say to them, "Go, open the gates of Gehenna and bring them forth." . . . At once Michael and Gabriel will open the forty thousand gates of Gehenna and bring them forth . . . and they will wash them and salve them and heal Gehenna's wounds and dress them in fine clothes and lead them into the presence of the Holy One Blessed Be He and all the righteous.

Zerubavel the son of She'altiel, a scion of the House of David prominent in the construction of the Second Temple in the age of Ezra, was associated in Jewish apocalyptic literature with the messiah by virtue of the prophet Haggai's declaration: "On that day [of judgment], says the Lord of Hosts, I will take you, Zerubavel the son of She'altiel my servant, and place you like a seal [over the people of Israel], for it is you whom I have chosen." What the Alphabet of Rabbi Akiva is depicting, then, is a session of aggadah at which the messiah loudly declaims the rabbis' kaddish. The inmates of Gehenna, hearing God's greatness invoked and acknowledging the justice of their punishment, say "Amen" with such fervor that God mercifully commutes their sentence and admits them to paradise, just as He did with Akiva's sinner.

By the end of Talmudic times, therefore, Judaism had arrived at the notion that prayer—and specifically, the rabbis' kaddish—could redeem the souls of the damned. From here, it was but a short conceptual step to the regular recital of this kaddish, minus its petition for the welfare of Torah scholars, by mourners. The actual custom, however, took root over a lengthy period. It appears first to have become a daily practice in thirteenth-century Germany, from where it spread gradually to the rest of Ashkenazi Europe and beyond. In the extensive glosses that he wrote on the *Shulhan Arukh*, Yosef Karo's contemporary, the Polish rabbi Moshe Isserles, speaks of the prayer as the daily rite of mourning that it is today throughout the Jewish world.

Saying the kaddish became so emotionally fraught because its neglect was taken to indicate indifference to the fate of the dead in the world-to-come and a willingness to abandon them to the sufferings of Gehenna. There is historical irony in this when one considers how opposed biblical Judaism was to the pagan practice of sacrifice and prayer for the dead, and to the belief that human intervention could improve their lot. Yet paganism, for all its deficiencies, addressed human needs that monotheistic faiths like Judaism, try as they might to ignore them, repeatedly discovered could not be repressed forever—and such was the need to feel there must be something one can do for those in the next world whom one has loved in this one. Already weakened in Talmudic times, biblical religion's view of the country of death as a realm beyond the influence of the living vanished entirely by the late Middle Ages.

Not all rabbis were fully comfortable with this. Isserles writes pointedly that reciting the three daily services in their entirety is "more useful" than saying the kaddish. He also observes that "the practice is to recite the kaddish for only eleven months, so as not to relate to one's father and mother as sinners, the sentence of the wicked [in Gehenna] being twelve months." This does not, to tell the truth, make perfect sense, for if one has such confidence in one's parents' virtue, why say the kaddish for them at all? Yet Isserles saw no point in resisting an already entrenched custom, even though he doubted it had special efficacy. The kaddish had become what it had become and nothing he might do was going to change that.

My mother died when I was forty-two, my father eight years later. Once the week of the shiva was over, I never said the kaddish for either of them.

I'm not sure my mother would have minded. Although the daughter of a rabbi, a leader of the religious Zionist movement in the years before the establishment of Israel, and the granddaughter of a renowned Lithuanian rabbinical scholar and yeshiva head, her religion was a casual affair. She conceived of it, I think, more as a matter of social circumstance than anything else. I first realized this as a boy one Saturday morning. As is common in Orthodox homes, our kitchen stove had a tin sheet placed over a burner left on a low flame, so that food could be warmed on the Sabbath without having to light a forbidden fire. I was passing the kitchen doorway when I saw my mother do the unimaginable. A draft must have blown out the flame, and unaware that she was being watched, she struck a match and relit it. I slipped away without being noticed and never mentioned what I saw, but I had seen it.

And my father? Had I asked him in the years before his mind was destroyed by Alzheimer's whether my saying the kaddish after his death was important to him, he might have denied it, but I would no more have believed him than I believed his denial, once he considered me old enough to confide in, of the existence of God. No God? To whom then was he pouring his heart out on those Saturday nights before the Havdalah candle was lit, that most melancholy time of the Jewish week, when I heard him alone in the darkness of his room, mournfully crooning the evening prayer? Pouring his heart out! *Ve'ahavatkha-a-a-a al tasir mimenu l'olami-im*, with that pleading falsetto rise on the last syllables: "And may Thy l-o-o-ove not depart from *us forever*"—whose love was that? The only answer he ever gave me to the question of why he regularly prayed every day was, "Because that's what a Jew does."

Saying the kaddish was what a Jew did, too. Why didn't I?

His death could not but be welcomed. Although the *viduy,* the deathbed confession, enjoins the dying man to pray, "May it be Your will that you cure me entirely, and if I die may my death be an atonement for all my sins," not even my father's dementia could have made him eager to be cured of the pneumonia he died from. The last years were terrible, though not without occasional comic relief. He had always been a legendary *ba'al korey*, a public reader of the Torah renowned for the exactitude and expressive clarity of his delivery, first for dozens of years in New York, at the synagogue of the Jewish Theological Seminary where he taught, and then in Jerusalem after he retired and moved to Israel with my mother. Even when his brain was in ruins, he remained astonishingly able to chant the weekly Torah portion so unerringly that members of the congregation who were unaware of his condition never guessed it. Once, when there was no one to accompany him to services, he set out for them by himself, lost his way, wandered into the wrong synagogue without realizing his mistake, and strode up to the Torah when the time came to read from it. Told that the congregation already had a Torah reader, he began to protest vociferously. Luckily, he was recognized by someone and escorted home.

His life had become a pointless insult. And yet when he lay dying in the hospital, struggling to breathe, I found myself, against all logic, cheering each breath. *Good! Another!* His chest rose and fell. *Another!* I waited. It didn't come. Was he dead? He breathed. *And another!* It wasn't me rooting for him, because I had no reason to want the mockery of a man he had become to go on living. It was the life in me for the life in him, life rooting for life. In death, we had a common foe.

But I wouldn't say the kaddish for him. Why not?

It wasn't that I didn't mourn him. The person I grieved for had disappeared long ago, but I had loved that person and he had loved me. He was the man who had taken me to baseball games when I was a child and sat patiently reading a book while I followed the play on the field, with whom I had walked home from the little *shul* in a residence hotel on West 103rd Street that we prayed in on Sabbath eves, my small hand in his big one, the tall buildings of Manhattan as peaceful as the wooden houses of the hamlet he had grown up in on the banks of the Dnieper, the world and my own heart at rest.

It wasn't the kaddish itself. I thought its words were magnificent. I had never understood the objection that they had nothing to do with death. They had everything to do with death, even if that was not their original purpose. They proclaimed the majesty of it all in the face of death, in defiance of death. They bore witness to this majesty's being greater than death.

It certainly wasn't lack of time. Clearly, I wasn't going to start attending synagogue every day. But the kaddish isn't an all-or-nothing obligation. Nothing in Jewish tradition ordains that if you miss it a hundred times, you mustn't say it the hundred-and-first. And I didn't.

Was I afraid of being roped in? It's cunning, the kaddish. Not by chance is it one of the few prayers in the liturgy that must be said in a *minyan*. "Come!" it says to the mourner who never has been an observant Jew. "Come back!" it says to the one who has been. "You can't do this by yourself. You need others. The door of the synagogue is open. There is no other."

Walk through it and you may stay. I've seen it happen. A death notice goes up in town and a week or two later I spot the mourner on his way to prayer, a newly grown beard on his cheeks. Fine. Thirty days without a trim, says Semahot, and not a few nonobservant Jews in Israel heed this out of filial piety. But then the month passes, I see the man again—and the beard has grown thicker. Not only that, there is now a *kipah* on his head. He has become a *hozer b'tshuvah,* a lost sheep returned to the fold.

Cunning. The kaddish gets you when you're down. You're stricken, vulnerable; you've imagined the sword of death on your own throat. The constant attention of the shiva is gone. And here, to make up for it, is a congregation that says amen and surrounds you with its solidarity and faith. Your father is dead; it's now your job to take his place by doing what he would have done. After thirty days, you're used to it; after a year, you may not want to give it up. Why should you, especially if you had it as a child and lost it and never thought you could have it back since, unlike your father, you wouldn't pray to a God you didn't believe in? In all those years, we had never once discussed my teenage lapse from observance. For two adult freethinkers, the subject was absurdly difficult.

Was that it? Not really. True, I sometimes did wonder whether abstaining from Judaism wasn't like being on the wagon: one drink and the habit would be back. But I didn't seriously think that was a danger. It was more a matter of pure willfulness. *Non serviam.*

I sometimes thought of those words during the year I wasn't saying the kaddish for my father. They're the Latin Bible's translation of a phrase from Jeremiah and they appear in James Joyce's *Ulysses.* In Joyce's earlier novel, *Portrait of the Artist as a Young Man,* the main character Stephen Dedalus breaks in adolescence with the Catholic faith he was raised in. Now, in his early twenties, Stephen is haunted by the recent death of his mother, whose last wish that he pray for her in accordance with the Catholic rites he refused to grant. "There is something sinister in you," his friend Buck Mulligan tells him in *Ulysses'* opening pages. "You wouldn't kneel down to pray for your mother on her deathbed when she asked you. Why? Because you have the cursed jesuit strain in you, only it's injected the wrong way." Stephen says nothing. Later that day, though, when his mother appears phantasmagorically and calls out, "Repent, Stephen! Prayer is all powerful," he answers: "*Non serviam*."

I will not serve. Was there something sinister in me, too? What perverse principle could make me think that saying the kaddish would compromise me? Didn't the gesture to my father matter more?

I will not serve. But Stephen's mother was alive. My father didn't know whether I was saying the kaddish for him or not. Why the foolish pangs of conscience?

I will not serve. These are also, as Stephen knows, the words attributed by Christian tradition to Lucifer, the proud angel of light. Refusing to do God's bidding, he was cast down from heaven with his fellow rebels and became Satan.

❧

I was not by my father's side when he died during the night. I learned of his death in the morning when I was asked, as a matter of protocol, to identify his body at the hospital morgue. Upon hearing such news, a Jew is supposed to say *barukh dayan emet*, "Blessed be the true judge," and the blessing in this case was real, if late in arriving. The drawer of a large refrigerator was opened and my father was pulled out, wrapped in a sheet. He didn't look peaceful, as the dead are often said to look. He looked angry and peevish, as if he had been beaten in a game he resented losing. His mouth hung open, caught in the middle of a last, unfinished breath.

The mouths of the dead are not to be left gaping. "The custom among Jews," writes Maimonides in his laws of the mourner, "is to shut the eyes of the deceased, tie his jaws, and seal his orifices after washing him and salving him with sweet unguents. His hair is cut and he is dressed in inexpensive shrouds sewn from white linen so as not to shame those who cannot afford better ones."

These are, more or less, the rules still followed in preparing a corpse for a Jewish burial. In Maimonides' day, this was done by the deceased's family, as it was for his brother by Shmuel Hanagid, who personally laid Yitzhak in the grave. This must have been dug, however, by others. Spanish Jews, according to Nahmanides, maintained volunteer associations responsible for the funeral arrangements, so that "once the mourner has finished preparing [the dead body], they take it to the graveyard and shoulder all responsibility for it."

By the sixteenth century, the associations spoken of by Nahmanides had spread to other countries, perhaps with the help of the Jews exiled from Spain in 1492. At first appearing in Italy and Germany, they went by the name of the *hevra kadisha*, "the holy society." In many places, they developed into powerful fraternal lodges that also cared for the sick and indigent, administered hospitals, asylums, and charities, and held public events such as annual banquets; then, as other institutions assumed these roles in modern times, they reverted to their original function. In Israel, unlike America, where one has the alternative of a funeral home, the Hevra Kadisha is a state-funded organization belonging to the ministry of religion and tasked with transporting all Jewish dead to a *tahara* or purification room and from there to the cemetery.

I wasn't there to see that happen. Twice while writing this book, I tried to attend a *tahara*. In Israel, I made contact with a hevra kadisha member who inquired on my behalf and reported back that the group's supervising rabbi would not countenance an observer at the ritual. It would be a violation, the rabbi said, of *k'vod ha-met*, the dignity of the dead. On a visit to New York, I was promised by someone I knew in a hevra kadisha in Manhattan that he would admit me to a *tahara* if one took place on his watch while I was there. It did, but at the last minute he phoned apologetically: his fellow volunteers had objected to my presence and he had to withdraw the invitation.

I accepted his offer to show me the facilities when not in use. Located in the basement of a synagogue, they resembled a small operating room. Bright overhead lights. Spotless tile walls. A gleaming white tile floor. Two stainless-steel tables on wheels with transparent, thick plastic tops, and between them, a toilet with a tall spigot and long rubber hose. Some buckets. A bathtub with an odd-looking contraption hanging over it: an electric motor from which a large wooden board was suspended by ropes. A garbage pail with a disposable bag. A sign saying "Please Keep This Tahara Room Clean."

The procedure was explained to me. As a rule, the dead body was handled by a team of four workers, all men if it was a male's, all women if a female's. It was laid on its back on one of the tables and a Hebrew prayer was recited that began: "Master of the Universe, have mercy on this dead person, _____ the son [or daughter] of _____ . . . . May his [or her] soul rest with the righteous and may You rescue him [or her] from all distress and from a day of evil [judgment] and from the sentence of Gehenna." It was then undressed and any bandages or dressings were cut away. Postmortem bleeding, if there was any, was stanched with a medical solution and the blood and absorbent cotton were kept to be buried with the body. This was next washed carefully from top to bottom, first on its right side and then on its left: one of the team poured water from a bucket into a pot, a second tipped it from the pot onto the corpse, a third cleansed, a fourth dried. Fingernails and toenails were cleaned with toothpicks; all polish was removed from them. Buckets containing nine *kabim* of water, a Talmudic measure, were poured over the corpse and the words *Tahor hu!* ("He is pure!") or *Tehora hi!* ("She is pure!") were chanted three times.

Next came the turn of the tub, which acted as a *mikveh* or ritual immersion pool. Placed on the board, the body was lowered into the water and raised three times by the motor, "*Tahor hu!*" being repeated again each time. From there it was returned to the table, dried, and dressed in its burial clothes. Modeled on the garments of the High Priest as described in the book of Leviticus, these included the *mitznefet,* a cowl that covered the face; loose-fitting cloth pants or *mikhnasayim;* the *k'tonet,* a tunic for the upper half of the body; and the *avnet,* a sash twisted three times before being knotted at the waist to form the Hebrew letter *shin* for Shaddai, God the All-Powerful. Fully dressed, the body was placed on a winding sheet in its coffin, which lay open on the second table. The sheet or shroud was wrapped around it and it was ready for burial.

The entire procedure took one to two hours. It sounded surgically precise. The room looked cold and clinical. Yet though the man showing it to me was a businessman who traveled frequently and valued his time when at home, he always made the effort to come when he could, despite being summoned on short notice and often forced to cancel previous plans. So did the others in his group. They depended on each other. If one didn't show up, the work was harder, especially if the body was a big one.

Dead bodies are heavy. I remember the time I had to help lift one. It was someone's who had just died and I wouldn't have known from its still undissipated warmth that it wasn't alive. I would have known from its weight, though. It weighed more than a body its size should have. Call it the soul, if you wish—call it the vital force—call it Aristotle's entelechy: all life's buoyancy had gone out of it.

And it was worse for the volunteers when the body was light, since that usually meant it was a child's. By the time they were done, they were physically and emotionally exhausted.

What made them do it? It wasn't a social thing. Conversation during a *tahara* was minimal; any trivial or unnecessary remark was unbefitting to *k'vod ha-met.* Another Hebrew term that came up in our discussion, one harder to translate, was *hesed shel emet.* Perhaps the best one can do would be "a selfless act of kindness." In the book of Genesis the words occur as *hesed v'emet,* "kindness and truth," in the verse in which the dying Jacob beseeches his son Joseph: "If I have found favor in your eyes . . . deal with me in kindness and truth. Bury me not, I pray you, in Egypt." On this, Genesis Rabba comments: "Why kindness *and* truth? Is there such a thing as kindness and lies? [There is, for] A saying goes, 'If it's your friend's son who has died, carry the body. If it's your friend, put it down.' "

This folk saying is nastily cynical. Help at the funeral of a friend's son, it advises, because you may want the favor returned; don't bother to help at his own funeral, because he's no longer alive to return it. A *hesed shel emet* is an act of kindness performed with no possible anticipation of reward—and hevra kadisha volunteers, it would seem, feel more impelled than others to perform such acts. What is more thankless than caring anonymously and without remuneration for someone who is not there to appreciate it?

Except that the dead *are* there, we are told by the early-seventeenth-century rabbi Aharon Berakhiah of Modena, whose book *Ma'avar Yabok,* "Crossing the Yabok," is yet another canonical Jewish text about death and dying. Its title comes from the story of Jacob's crossing the Yabok River on the eve of his fateful confrontation with his brother Esau, and living in post-Renaissance Italy, whose educated Jews often had a knowledge of classical culture, Berakhiah may have been thinking of the analogy with the Styx of Greek mythology. A kabbalist of the Lurianic school in search of the mystical truths behind the outward details of Jewish ritual, he writes that the soul stays by the body until it is buried. It is aware of everything that is said and done in the *tahara* room, in which "a kindness done to the body is also a kindness done to the soul." Part of the *tahara*'s purpose, indeed, is to help the soul part from the body, because "a dead person knows more about the affairs of this world before being cleansed than afterward." His purification "draws him and his soul away from the material sphere," and once the body has been immersed in the *mikveh,* the soul abandons its desire to return to it and "aspires to don the garments of the light of paradise."

My soul will be at my *tahara*, then, watching my body as it is washed and dressed. Feeling it, too, as an amputee feels a phantom limb: the sluice of water over its face, the washcloth probing its armpits and groin, the voices saying "Over here," "Help me with this leg," "Turn it that way," the sudden shock of being plunged into the tub. And again. And a third time. *Tahor hu.* Thank God that's over.

But I do feel the kindness of it. These men mean well by me. I'm grateful to have the detritus of dying washed away, like sweat by a shower after a hard day's work. It's not their fault their hands are rougher than a woman's.

I wish they were a woman's. I wish they were my mother's, the hands that washed me as a child. Careful and competent, they soaped me, scrubbed me, shampooed me while I wriggled and squirmed. I wish they could do it now.

At my mother's funeral, I gave the eulogy. I don't remember all that I said. I do remember quoting the verse *sheker ha-hen v'hevel ha-yofi,* "Comeliness is a lie and beauty is vanity, but the woman who fears the Lord, she shall be praised." It comes from the last chapter in Proverbs, a paean beginning *eshet hayil mi yimtsa,* "a woman of valor who shall find," that is traditionally declaimed by a husband to his wife at the Friday night table. My father never missed saying it. He knew its twenty verses by heart and looked across the table at my mother as he chanted them.

I remember saying that my mother had not especially feared the Lord. I said that her comeliness was no lie and her beauty no vanity, and that I wished to praise her for them. The lie, I said, was old age's. It was sickness and death's.

They struck comeliness down and blotted beauty out. They made us forget they had ever existed. That was the lie.

For a year, I had watched my mother decline. A minor heart condition, the result of rheumatic fever in childhood, had turned into a major one. She had trouble walking up the hill to the bus stop from her and my father's Jerusalem apartment; she could no longer climb the stairs to it by herself; she was bedridden; she needed an oxygen mask to breathe; she had mini-strokes. One day she fell on her way to the bathroom. I raised her nightgown to inspect the large black-and-blue mark already forming on the side of her thigh and was forced to see the naked shabbiness of her body before I turned my face away. "Take me to my seat," she said. "*Es fängt an.*" In her mind she had fallen on the stairs of the opera, in Berlin. That's where she had gone in 1929 to get her master's degree in social work, after graduating from Hunter College in New York. Berlin had the reputation of being the world's most libertine city in those days. "You people think you invented sin," she once sniffed at me in my college years during a generational argument about social mores.

She had always been an elegant woman—a tasteful dresser, a deft housekeeper, a gracious hostess to the guests who were often in our home, a skilled professional admired by her fellow workers. When she was young she was very pretty, with large dark eyes. She had a black lamb's wool coat that she wore with a beret, and she wore it one winter's day when we walked down Broadway to Schrafft's. That was a fancy soda-fountain establishment to which she sometimes took me for the hot-fudge sundaes that were her special treat for me. They came in tall glass goblets with a long, thin spoon to get to the bottom of them, and I would sit licking the fudge from the spoon on one of the high stools by the counter, swinging my feet that didn't reach the floor. On our way home we stopped by a store window. I don't remember what was in it. "Look," my mother said to me gaily. "Look how pretty that is!" Why has this moment remained with me? Perhaps because she looked so grand in her lamb's wool coat. Perhaps because she was not generally an emotionally expressive woman. Perhaps because the six-year-old trying to see what she saw had seen a hidden side of her instead. Perhaps because he was happy.

The worst part of her dying for me was that I could no longer visualize the mother I had had. Between us now was a screen on which flickered constant images of someone old and sick. I couldn't push it aside or get beyond it. It was a roadblock barring my way to her.

Sheker ha-hen v'hevel ha-yofi! My voice cracked. "Eulogizing the dead is of great value," writes Berakhiah,

> because the tears produced by it pry open the gates of tears in the upper world—gates that stand apart from the gates of stern justice. It is said that even when every gate is locked, the gates of tears are not. Yet [for this to be true] the weeping must be for the fate of the soul, not for the fate of the material body, as is the weeping of foolish women.

I wept like a foolish woman.

There is no single designated site, or even time, for Jewish eulogies. When Judah the Prince died, we are told, they were given for an entire year in synagogues and houses of study throughout Palestine and Babylonia. Other traditional places for them have been by the entrance to the cemetery and at the graveside; with the advent of motor transportation, more distant funeral chapels have become venues, too. It is also now common for the single eulogy to be replaced by a series of remarks made by the deceased's family and friends. There is something democratically appealing about this: let whoever wants to speak, speak. Yet there is also the danger that not everything spoken will augment the moment. Those attending a funeral have their private emotions and memories of the person who has died. These are not necessarily enhanced by the private emotions and memories of others.

Still, isn't this better than the congregational rabbi who, not having known the dead person well or at all, delivers an encomium based on hastily gathered bits of information and the obligation to spare no praise? There is a joke about such a eulogizer enumerating the virtues of the deceased. The dead man, he proclaims, was a wonderful husband and father, dearly loved by his wife and children. He was a loyal friend, liked and admired by all. He was an outstanding Jew, devoted to his community. He was a generous one, too, an unstinting giver to charity. As he is speaking, the rabbi notices the corpse signaling to him. Although he tries to ignore it, its motions grow more insistent until he is forced to lean in its direction. "Rabbi," it whispers, "don't forget to mention my modesty."

I first heard this joke from a relative, a Habad Hasid, and Habad is unique in the Jewish world in forbidding eulogies at funerals. The rationale for this is that one must strive to be truthful and a eulogy is no place for truth-telling. *De mortuis nil nisi bonum,* the Latin proverb states, "About the dead, only good [is to be said]," of which the witty Jewish equivalent is *aharey mot k'doshim emor,* "After a death, say 'holy'"—a phrase composed of the names of three successive Torah readings in the book of Leviticus: *Aharey mot,* which begins, "After the death of the two sons of Aaron"; *K'doshim,* which begins, "And God said to Moses, 'Speak to the congregation of the children of Israel and say to them, ye shall be holy'"; and *Emor,* which begins, "And God said to Moses, 'Say to the priests, the sons of Aaron.'" Perhaps this was why my father, who grew up in a Habad home, did not wish to eulogize my mother, though I think he was too devastated to do so in any case.

And so I took it upon myself, in a hall by the cemetery gate. From there, my mother's body was borne on a stretcher to its grave. I walked behind it with my father and sister while a hevra kadisha member led from in front and dolefully declaimed the words of the first-century Akavya ben Mehalalel:

> Think of three things and you will be kept from sin. Know where you come from, and where you are going, and to whom you will owe an accounting. Where do you come from? From a putrid drop. And where are you going? To a place of dirt, worms, and maggots. And to whom will you owe an accounting? To the king of kings, the Holy One Blessed Be He.

This is strong stuff. Putrid? The spermatozoon with whose brave dash for the sanctuary of the womb my mother's life and all our lives began? And yet walking behind her draped body that looked so paltry and insubstantial, nothing in me rose to protest. How pitiful it all was.

Berakhiah seeks to give the funeral procession a transcendent meaning with the help of a play on words. The stretcher bearers, he writes, are like the Levites who carried the Holy Ark when the Tabernacle was disassembled and moved in the desert. Carrying the dead is "taking part in the secret meaning of [the verse in Exodus] 'And they brought the Tabernacle [*mishkan*] to Moses,' for the tabernacle when it travels is [like] the soul that was put in pawn [*memushkenet*] in this lowly world against its will" and is now, redeemed by its Owner, returning to its home on high. "Just as [the pallbearers] accompany the body in its descent [to the grave] with their own bodies, so they should focus their thoughts on accompanying its *nefesh* with their own *nefesh*, and its *ru'ah* with their own *ru'ah*, and its *neshamah* with their own *neshamah*, for the *nefesh, ruah,* and *neshamah* of the dead escort the body to the grave." Even the pallbearers' rest stops have a hidden significance. Each time they pause or are spelled on their way, the demonic forces attracted to the dead are driven off, since "the evil spirits have permission to roam [through the world] but not to rest." The spirits are, one might say, like flies following a delivery cart of meat: they buzz on when it halts.

The procession stopped the prescribed seven times on its way to my mother's grave. It did not circle her body the same number of times when the grave was reached, as ultra-Orthodox Jews do. Berakhiah compares this to the sevenfold circling of the walls of Jericho by the army of Joshua, but it bears an even more striking resemblance to the seven circles made by the bride around the groom at some, mostly Orthodox, weddings, underscored by the funereal music to which wedding bands switch at that moment. One wonders which ritual came first. Is the wedding disguised as a funeral to confuse the Evil Eye, which is jealous of the bride and groom's good fortune? Or are the shrouds of the corpse, which in death has surrendered the soul to God's embrace, comparable to a wedding sheet?

Next came the *keri'ah,* the ritual tearing of our garments, and the *tsidduk ha-din* or "vindication of judgment," recited by the leader of the procession. "Wear something old," my wife reminded me when I was dressing that morning. This is advice that most mourners follow, even if it is not quite in the spirit of things; for if one cannot bear to have something new, let alone one's favorite shirt, sweater, or coat, slashed by a knife, how deep can one's grief be said to run? And yet what is done by everyone embarrasses no one, and Judaism is a religion that is adept at mitigating its own stringencies.

In its simplest form, which is the verse from Deuteronomy, "The Rock, His work is perfect, for all His ways are just; a faithful God who does no wrong, righteous and fair is He," the *tsidduk ha-din* goes back to Talmudic times. The rest of the prayer consists of medieval verses. They make the same point that Deuteronomy does: God does not make mistakes and we must acknowledge His justice. I prefer the kaddish. It does not say God is just. It says He is beyond all blessing, song, praise, and consolation. This is the difference between Job's comforters and Job. The comforters insist that God must have good reasons for what He has done to Job. Job refuses to be convinced. He is still refusing when along comes a howling storm and blows away all reasons, convictions, notions of causality, beliefs in God's justice, and presumptions that God owes anyone an accounting. God is beyond all that. God is the Grandeur, and the Wonder, and the Terror, and say: amen.

❧

As is the custom in Israel, my mother was laid in the ground in only her shrouds. Contact with the soil of the Land of Israel is meritorious: this was taught by Judah the Prince. In keeping with such a belief, my grandmother, like other pious Jews of her and previous generations, kept a cloth pouch of earth from Palestine in her chest of drawers in the Bronx, to be put in the grave with her.

Some Israelis complain that they would like to be buried in a coffin like Diaspora Jews, but the soil of the Land of Israel is good enough for me. I've tended my garden in it. I've hoed it, shoveled it, raked it, spaded it, broken its rocks with a pickaxe, pried them out of it with my bare hands, carried it in buckets, trundled it in wheelbarrows, shaken it out of my boots and shoes. I'm a dirt lover. I like poking my fingers into it, getting it under my nails. I like the sleek plumpness of the worms that romp in it when it's wet and sticky with rain. Why snub them for the solitary confinement of a wooden box? Let them grow plumper on me. Let the moles swerve around me as they hammer out their tunnels with the false foreheads of their downward-swiveled skulls. For dust thou art and to dust thou shalt return, God tells Adam. Let it be dust.

But the canvas scuttles of yellow earth lined up by mother's grave were hard to look at. One after another, they would be dumped on her. That's how you plant a tree, I told myself. You dig a hole, and you pile the earth from it alongside it, and you slide the sapling from its container into the bottom of the hole, and you shovel the earth back in, one shovelful at a time. True. But the tree will grow.

And when the pallbearers tilted their stretcher and my mother slid into her grave like a little boat from its launching slip, I drew a sharp breath. So this was it. This was what it all came to. They emptied the scuttles, handed new ones as quickly as they flung the used ones aside. They worked quickly and smoothed their work out with a hoe when they were done.

There remained the kaddish and the *el maley rahamim*. After the kaddish, the *el maley rahamim*, "God, full of Mercy," is probably the prayer most associated with Jewish mourning, and even more than the kaddish, it's a recent arrival in the Jewish liturgy. Ascribed to the Moravian rabbi Yom Tov Lippman Heller, its words are said to have been composed in the wake of the massacres of Jews in the Ukraine in 1648–49. The notes they're sung to don't add up to a melody. They aren't a chant. They're the *Sprechgesang* of cantorial music, starting as a long, tremulous, minor-key sob (*God full of mercy, who dwelleth on high*) and gathering confidence (*in the ranks of the purest of saints who shine with the brightness of the heavens*) until they turn into a demand, confident of its right to what it is asking: *grant perfect peace on the wings of Thy presence to the soul of Shulamit, the daughter of Meir and Bella, who has gone to another world.*

My mother.

And whereas we pray for the ascent of her soul, may she repose in paradise and the Merciful One shelter her forever in the fastness of His wings and bind her soul in the bond of life.

Then, though, it ebbs and expires with a fading, operatic sigh, a rueful admission that God will do as He pleases:

The Lord is her lot and may she rest in peace in her resting place, and say: amen.

The hevra kadisha leader apologized to my mother:

"Shulamit, the daughter of Meir and Bella, we ask your forgiveness. Although we may not have accorded you the full respect due you, we did everything according to the custom of our holy land. Be a true intercessor for all Israel. Go in peace, and rest in peace in your resting place, and may you arise to your fate at the End of Days."

The funeral was over. Whoever wished to lay a pebble on my mother's grave before departing did so. No one seems to know where this custom comes from. It may be the oldest of all Jewish burial rites. Rocks and stones litter the hills of Palestine, and in Genesis we read of *matseyvot* or stone cairns erected to commemorate significant events, such as Jacob and Laban's pact of peace, or to mark the site of a grave like Rachel's. In post-biblical times, this custom disappeared and the word *matseyvah* came to signify a grave's headstone. The pebbles may be the shrunken remnants of the biblical cairn, a symbolic vestige preserved long after what it symbolized had been forgotten.

Nowadays, some Jews adopt the Gentile practice of laying wreaths of flowers on graves. These seem loud and gaudy compared to the simple sobriety of pebbles. A pebble says: *I cost nothing.* It says: *You'll find me everywhere.* It says: *I mean what you wish me to mean.*

The shiva. I hated it.

It's said to be a wise custom. No doubt it is. For a week, the mourner or mourners are embraced by friends and acquaintances who see to their needs, surround them with warmth and sympathy, and help prevent their being over-whelmed by strong feelings that they might have trouble coping with on their own. Not long ago I read an essay in a contemporary volume on Jewish mourning that com-pared the shiva to the "holding environment" of a psy-choanalytic session. Just as the analyst, the author wrote, functions "as a reliable, available, potentially empathic presence," so the shiva creates "an emotionally protective setting" in which "the mourner is permitted to express and experience the self in a way that mimics many aspects of the psychoanalytic holding situation."

But I didn't want a psychoanalytic holding situation. I wanted to be left alone. My mother had died. My immedi-ate reaction was not a strong sense of loss or grief. It was a heavy, bitter sadness that this was the way it had to end. I didn't want to talk about it. I didn't want to be distracted from it. I wanted to feel it unhindered.

Servabam. I sat for a week with my father and sister in my parents' apartment while the condolence callers came from morning till night. We did not observe all the rules, such as sitting on low stools, continuing to dress in our torn funeral garments, and wearing socks or slippers instead of shoes. We did eat a *seu'dat havra'ah,* a "meal of recovery" prepared by the neighbors when we came home from the cemetery, and we kept to the bounds of the apart-ment without leaving it, and we had two daily *minyans.* The leather thongs of the tefillin of *shaharit* bit into my arm like a bittersweet memory.

It was an ordeal. My parents were a highly social cou-ple, even though I sometimes think that were it not for my mother, my father would have been happy to live like a hermit with his books; they knew a large number of people, mostly from the Jerusalem academic world, and nearly all felt obliged to come. Some I knew, some I didn't. All had to be talked to, made to feel welcome and appreciated, thanked when they departed. Some shook hands or murmured a few words when they left. The religiously observant said, "*Ha-makom yenahem etkhem b'tokh she'ar aveley tsiyon v'yerushalyim, velo tosifu l'da'avah od*"—"May the Almighty comfort you among the other mourners of Zion and Jerusalem, and may you know no more sorrow." By the end of each day, I felt drained.

This is not, of course, the theory of it. In theory, the mourner isn't supposed to have to do any of this. No one at a shiva, writes Maimonides, is even allowed to speak to the mourner unless the mourner speaks first. An excellent provision. But in practice, you can't just sit there in silence. And if you try to, another essay in the same volume, entitled "The Art of Making a Shiva Call," instructs the caller what to do:

> Simply offering a hug, a kiss, a handshake, an arm around the shoulder, speaks volumes. If you do want to open a conversation, start with a simple "I'm so sorry" or "I don't know what to say. This must be so difficult for you" or "I was so sorry to hear about ____." . . . Recall something personal: "I loved _____. Remember the times we went on vacation together? She adored you so much." . . . Spend anywhere from a few moments to ten minutes with the mourners. There will be others who will always want to speak with them, and you can always come back.

The callers at my mother's shiva were not so gauche or officious, though some did go on sitting there a good deal longer than ten minutes. Not all were friends of my parents; my friends and my sister's friends came, too. But the apartment was small, and even if you wanted to talk to someone it wasn't possible with all the comings and goings and the person in the next chair, who kept changing, overhearing what you said. It wasn't anyone's fault. I just wanted to be alone.

And that's what Judaism didn't want me to be. It didn't trust me to be alone. It saw no value in aloneness. It didn't agree with Plotinus that the soul's path to God was the flight of the alone to the Alone.

A wise religion. It surrounds us with rules and regulations and commandments and communal structures to keep us out of trouble. And we *are* trouble. We're attracted to it. We'll get into it time and again if left to ourselves.

You might be knocked down by a death and want to get up on your own and discover when no one is around to help you that you can't do it. The shiva is there to make sure this doesn't happen, at least not in mourning's first days.

I had served. When I said goodbye to my father before heading home from Jerusalem, he asked which side of the Hudson I was planning to drive on. It was the first sign that his mind was beginning to go.

Where am I? Someone is beating me. "What is your name?" he shouts. My mouth is full of dirt and it's hard to speak. This is terrible. I have forgotten other people's names in my life—more and more of them as I've grown older—but never my own. "Your name, your name!" shouts my assailant.

❧

There is a well-known tale by Y. L. Peretz, the Yiddish and Hebrew short-story writer and dramatist, about a soul. A Jew has died and his soul ascends to the heavenly tribunal for judgment. The prosecutor, defense counsel, and judges convene, a scale is placed before them, and two sacks are carried into the courtroom, one containing all the good deeds performed by the deceased while on earth, the other all the bad deeds. The sacks are emptied onto the balance pans, which drift slowly up and down, the good deeds now outweighing the bad ones, the bad ones now outweighing the good ones. When the last deeds have been shaken from the sacks, the pans balance exactly: there's not a hair's breadth between them. The soul can't enter heaven because it hasn't enough good deeds to its credit. It can't be sent to hell because it hasn't enough bad ones. What's to be done? The judges consult and hand down their verdict: the soul is sentenced to be a vagabond, wandering homelessly through the universe until God takes pity on it.

A prologue to the main body of the story, which relates how the wandering soul is delivered from its punishment, this scene is based on Hasidic folklore with its tales of the *olam ha-tohu,* the limbo-like "world of the void" through which souls can be made to roam ghost-like (a medieval notion probably influenced by the Catholic concept of purgatory), and of the scales of divine justice. In a story attributed to the eighteenth-century Hasidic master Mordecai of Neshkhiz, a traveler loses his way in a forest, enters a mysterious castle, and is threatened there with a cruel death unless he can provide proof of his virtue. A scale is brought and his deeds are weighed; alas, the bad ones weigh more. Just as his throat is about to be slit, an unknown figure runs up and throws a heavy overcoat on the pan of good deeds, driving it down and saving the traveler. Asked who he is, the figure replies: "Don't you remember me? I was the poor, homeless wretch you gave a ride to in your carriage one snowy winter night on a lonely road and covered with your overcoat because he was shivering from cold. Just now I was waked from my sleep in the grave and told to hurry to this place and throw the coat on the scale, and so I did."

Is the dead man a ghost or an actual, risen body? Perhaps he is the dead man's *nefesh,* his vital soul, which remains with the body, according to Berakhiah, after its passional and intellectual souls have departed. A belief in the dead's ongoing presence in the grave even as they dwell in other worlds or haunt this one exists in many cultures. No doubt this is why some visitors to cemeteries feel they can commune with the dead and even talk to them. We had a neighbor in town whose wife died years before him. Every Friday until his own death, he went to the cemetery, swept her grave, tended to the greenery around it, and sat beside it. Although I never asked him about this, he was clearly not just obeying a habit or a ritual.

But visiting the grave is a ritual in Judaism, too. Traditionally, it is performed by mourners after rising from the shiva; again a month after the funeral; and a third time with the passing of a year. On one of these occasions—it can be any of the three—the tombstone is unveiled. On all of them, the kaddish is recited and Psalms are read; there is a custom of spelling the deceased's Hebrew name by reciting a Psalm that begins with each letter of it. In the years that follow, this is done annually on the *yortsayt.* There is also a tradition of visiting graves in Elul, the Hebrew month at summer's end that precedes the High Holy Days. Another of Sholem Aleichem's "Railroad Stories" begins:

> "So you're off to the festivities and I'm coming back from them! I've just finished crying my heart out and you're about to begin. . . . But why don't I make some room for you? Here, move over this way. You'll be more comfortable."
>
> "Ah, that's better!"
>
> So two passengers sat chatting behind me in the car. That is, one did the talking while the other murmured an occasional word. . . .
>
> By now I understood what sort of "festivities" were being talked about. It was, I realized, the beginning of the penitential month of Elul with its midnight prayers, that sad but dear time of year when Jews travel to visit long-dead parents, children, and relatives. Pining mothers, orphaned daughters, mourning sisters, plain grief-stricken women—all go to have a good cry at the graves of their loved ones, where they let out their sorrow and ease the bitter burden of an afflicted heart.

Pilgrimages to the graves of revered rabbis have also been a feature of Jewish folk religion. Some of these, such as the *hilulot* of the Jews of Morocco, developed into real festivities, fetes accompanied by singing, dancing, and feasting. The main such event in today's Jewish world is the annual Lag b'Omer *hilulah* at the tomb of Shim'on bar Yohai on Mount Meron in the Galilee, which attracts hundreds of thousands of participants. Well attended, too, is the Rosh Hashanah pilgrimage to the burial site of Rabbi Nahman of Bratslav in the Ukrainian city of Uman. Gatherings of this sort do not commemorate a death. They pay homage to a life that exerts its power even from the grave.

Such hagiolatry was influenced by Christianity, and even more by Islam. Yet if Jews have had their saints and saints' tombs like Catholics and Muslims, they have refrained on the whole from the Catholic and Muslim veneration of relics, most scrupulously in the matter of body parts. Judaism knows no revered heads of St. Catherine or tongues of St. Anthony, no hairs from Muhammad's beard or teeth from his mouth. A Jew's every tooth and hair must be buried with the rest of him. After terrorist bombings in Israel, hevra kadisha members crawl on all fours over sidewalks and streets, searching for finger joints, ear lobes, and smaller bits of tissue to inter with the bodies they were blasted away from.

I know of no other people that goes to such lengths to recover its dead. For years after the Yom Kippur War, Israel's chaplaincy corps combed the sands of Sinai practically grain by grain in search of the bodies of soldiers killed in action. Following the disappearance of the submarine *Dakar* in the eastern Mediterranean in 1968, the Israeli navy conducted twenty-six different search missions in the hope of retrieving the remains of the crew until the craft's broken hull was located at a depth too far down for divers to reach. Israeli governments have made the return of one or two Jewish bodies a condition for the freeing of hundreds of convicted Palestinian terrorists.

"May you not be brought to a Jewish grave" is a time-honored Jewish imprecation. Israel is a country in which there is not only a universally observed taboo on cremation, but something close to a horror of it. Secular Israelis who think nothing of eating pork or not fasting on Yom

Kippur are instinctively repelled by the thought of their
bodies being incinerated after death. An association with
the chimneys of the Nazi death camps may have something to do with it, but surely a deeper matter is involved.
"Lo, I am gathered unto my people," says Jacob says to his
sons. "Bury me with my fathers." It's as old as the Bible,
even if the Bible is a book one hasn't read. And perhaps
there is also an unconscious Pascal's wager at work. *Yes,
of course, all that religious talk about resurrection is primitive
nonsense . . . but suppose . . . well, you can't prove mathemat-
ically that there isn't a one-in-a-million chance that it's true,
can you?* What is there to lose by waiting it out in the grave
rather than as ashes vanished on the wind?

Cemeteries are peaceful places when they are not too
busy or too large. (I was once in one near Tel Aviv in which
the funerals were serially announced over a loudspeaker
like departing suburban trains.) So, though, are dead-letter
offices. Others may have different experiences, but every
message I've tried sending to or via a grave has come back
with the stamp "Forwarding address unknown." The year
my mother died, I went to her grave the three prescribed
times and never returned. It was the same with my father.
Possibly this is a family trait, because I don't remember either of my parents visiting their own parents' graves, either.

Still, who doesn't fantasize about hearing from the dead?
Mediums and manufacturers of Ouija boards make a living
from this. Judaism frowns upon such things, just as it did
on King Saul's midnight ride to En-Dor. This doesn't, however, preclude other arrangements. A Hasidic story told by
the nineteenth-century Rabbi Yitzhak Eisig of Kumarna relates how, as a young man, he promised a fatally ill friend to
raise his small son, asking in return that the friend inform

him what happened to him after his death. The two sealed their pledge with a solemn handshake and Yitzhak Eisig brought the boy up devotedly, teaching him Torah and arranging when he came of age for his marriage to a bride from a wealthy and pious family. All this time, however, the boy's dead father failed to keep his promise. Before the wedding, over which he was to preside, Yitzhak Eisig, now a renowned Hasidic rabbi, disappeared. Rejoining the wedding guests just in time to conduct the ceremony, he told them at the banquet that followed:

As the time for the wedding approached, I went to my room and said, "I will not take my place beneath the wedding canopy until it is revealed to me from heaven what has kept my friend from honoring his pledge." And indeed, at the last moment he appeared to me while I was fully awake, looking like any living person. He came toward me and I asked: "What's taken you so long? Thirteen years have gone by without your doing what you said you would." "Here I am," he said. "I've come to tell you everything from the time my soul left my body until now."

The friend related:

When my soul departed, I felt no pain or sorrow. It was like drawing a thread from a pitcher of milk. The next thing I knew, I had fallen into a deep, peaceful sleep. When the hevra kadisha came to attend to me and started shifting me about, I wanted to rise and make them go away, but I couldn't move my body and I lay there like a log. I thought I was in my bed and dreaming it all. After the *tahara* and burial, once everyone at the funeral had left, I decided to rise from my grave. "I'm still alive," I told myself. "What am I doing in a graveyard?" But though I made up my mind to go home, I couldn't find the gate leading out of the cemetery.

The friend only realizes he is dead when seized and brought before the heavenly tribunal. There, he is told that despite all his merits, a single sin in his record rules out his immediate entry into paradise. The penance he is sentenced to is a detention cell from which he can view both the delights of the Garden of Eden and the torments of Gehenna, alternating endlessly between longing for the one place and dread of the other. Now, his time served, he has at last been given permission to honor his pledge. Yitzhak Eisig's story concludes:

> All this my friend told me while I sat in my room, after which he asked for a signed statement that he had kept his share of the bargain and was under no further obligation. . . . "Don't detain me in this world any longer," he said. "May God bless my son and safeguard him and shine His countenance upon him, but now let me be on my way. You cannot imagine how great are the delights of heaven. Even he who has only seen them from afar and had but the barest taste of them can no longer value a single one of this world's pleasures."

I wasn't in a waking state like Yitzhak Eisig of Kumarna when my mother appeared to me. For a year or two after her death, I hadn't been able to find a way back to her. All I saw when I tried was the same drawn, exhausted woman with oxygen tubes in her nose. On her thigh, where I had lifted her nightgown, a dark blotch spread over flabby flesh.

The nakedness of thy mother shalt thou not uncover; she is thy mother; thou shalt not uncover her nakedness. And I had uncovered it.

In my dream, I was a boy again. Six years old? Seven? Maybe eight. I was at home by myself, in our West End Avenue apartment. It was a winter night when it got dark early. Hungry, I went to the refrigerator to look for something to eat. When I opened it, it was empty. Completely bare except for one shriveled leaf of lettuce, blackening at the edges, lying on the bottom shelf.

The hopelessness of that shriveled leaf! I stared at it, not knowing what to do.

Just then a key turned in the front door. Of all the sounds of my childhood, this was the one I always waited for the most. I ran from the kitchen to the hall. My mother was standing in the doorway, young and radiant in her black lamb's wool coat. Bright with the flush of the winter cold, she held out her arms and I flung myself into them.

"Mommy," I said, my tears of joy wetting her coat.

CHAPTER FIVE

I am in our kitchen with my wife, my eldest daughter,
her husband, and their two-year-old son. There is a rat
in the kitchen sink. I run to the sink and try killing it by
hitting it over the head with a heavy cutting board. But
the rat, I now see, is a wild boar—and there is no need
to kill it, because it is slowly being eaten; it is in terrible,
piteous agony. Beside it is the beast that is devouring it.
This is a transparent leopard, a leopard without its skin,
all glowing red veins and pink flesh. Slim and aristocratic, it arches its catlike back and continues calmly to eat
the boar alive.

In the dream journal that I keep, I noted:

Either in the dream itself, or immediately upon waking,
it is clear to me that the leopard is death. A few weeks
ago, I killed a rat in the kitchen sink. The other night the
wild boars overturned the garbage can again.

The boars began turning up around our house over ten
years ago. There had always been boars in the valley below
us, but they rarely ventured farther up. Now they became

a nuisance, digging up gardens, smashing the branches of trees to get at fruit they couldn't reach, strewing garbage all over the street. A danger, too. One morning I found a neighbor's dog dead in our driveway, a puncture hole drilled to its heart.

Suppose it had been a child? They're fearsome-looking, wild boars. The big ones are almost as tall as calves, but they aren't built like calves. They're built like tanks, all bristling muscle and tusk. They're the dark, feral color of rats. Ordinary fences can't keep them out. What they can't knock down, they'll dig under.

A boar ripped apart a small fig tree I had nursed back from its roots after it was attacked by weevils. "If we can't stop them, we'll have to sell this house and move," I said to my wife.

In my journal I wrote:

> The boar in the dream is life, brute life, its sheer, unstoppable force—but the Leopard of Death is far stronger.

In the end, we put up an electrified fence around our property. It gives a nasty shock but no worse and is switched on by an automatic clock at dusk, when the boars start their day, and switched off again at dawn. Since then, they've kept away.

We still talk about selling the house, though. Sooner or later, I suppose we'll do it.

That will be hard. We've lived in it for over forty years. We designed it together with the architect. We were young

when we moved into it. It's painful to think of living any-
where else.

There have been times away from it, of course. But that's
what's so dreamlike about traveling. You're like a soul away
from its body. It's magical to be free of it as long as you
know it's there to come back to. The key that fits the lock,
the familiar door opening, the light switch found unerringly in the dark: it's like awaking in the morning and slipping back into all the parts of you. You lie in bed like someone returned from a journey, going from room to room.
Your legs, your arms, your hands, your chest, your head:
they're all there, just as you left them. It's good to be home.

There was a time when I thought of our home as built
for the ages. The daughters who had grown up in it would
inherit it. Their children would inherit it from them. There
was enough land in the back to build more on. It had been
cheap when we bought it. The town was little more than a
large village and we were practically the first outsiders to
choose to live in it for no other reason than that we liked it.
"What made you come here?" the locals asked suspiciously.
We explained: the air, the view, the nearby sea, the run-
down charm of the place. "Yes, yes," they said. "But what
made you come?"

Today, it's no longer a place where everyone knows everyone and a walk to the grocery involves a half-dozen
social encounters. It's a bedroom community, complete
with apartment buildings and suburban streets. The country has grown and the town has grown even faster, beyond anything we might have imagined. Most of the wild-
life that once roamed our property is gone: the hedgehogs,
the tortoises, the mongooses, the snakes, the polecats, the

porcupines that left their quills as calling cards. Even the scorpions. Everything but the rats and the boars. There are more of them than ever. And the jackals that wail at night like souls in hell.

Our daughters live in Tel Aviv and don't want to move back. Even if they did, it wouldn't make sense. The land we bought for thousands because no one else wanted it is now worth millions to a contractor. You don't live on that kind of property unless you already have that kind of money. We're getting older and it's harder each year to take care of it. Sooner or later, we'll sell. The contractor will knock down our home and build row houses like the ones already going up around us. It will take him an hour to demolish it and the rest of the day to clear away the rubble.

Still, I think I'd prefer that to a stranger living in our house. *Someone else in my house?* There might as well be someone else in my body.

It will definitely be a kind of dying.

One March evening, many years after my father's death, I went to synagogue for the first time to say the kaddish for him on his *yortsayt,* impelled by a nagging sense of a duty unperformed.

I felt nothing. There were several other kaddish-sayers besides me—whether year-long mourners or *yortsayt* observers, I couldn't tell—and they said the prayer at a rapid, practiced clip that forced me to rush to keep up with them. There was no time to concentrate on the words. Sometimes, I thought as I walked home, better never than late.

The next morning I rose early. It was a quarter to four. Outside it was raining. I dressed in darkness to keep from waking my wife. But the living room, when I stepped into it, shutting the bedroom door behind me, was full of light. The light came from the *yortsayt* candle lit for my father the night before. It stood on a low bookcase at the room's far end, a standard item that can be bought in any Israeli grocery store or supermarket, a small can of wax with a wick that burns for twenty-four hours. It lit the room with a soft luminosity that spread from its source like droplets of scent borne on air, and I thought: how much light one little wick gives.

I went over to it. Although the windows were shut tightly, the flame danced back and forth in its pool of melted wax as if something would not let it keep still. Back and forth across the surface of the pool: something would not let it keep still. "A candle of the Lord is the soul of man," says the book of Proverbs. In Hebrew, a *yortsayt* candle is a *ner neshamah*, a "soul candle."

A candle burns and goes out. This one, too, would sputter and choke at the end of the day. It would contract to a small red spark, flare up tenaciously, shrink to a tiny ember, darken to a sooty black dot. I thought of my father, fighting for each breath in the hospital, and I found myself saying the kaddish again, this time at my own pace.

One more rite completes the roster: *yizkor.* Four times a year—on Yom Kippur, on the last day of Sukkot, on the last day of Passover, and on Shavu'ot—it is observed in

synagogues before the Torah, a silent witness to the pro-
ceedings, is returned to the Ark.

The word *yizkor* comes from the Hebrew verb *zakhar,* "to
remember." It is the first word of a prayer having different
versions. In old Ashkenazi prayer books (*yizkor* is not part
of the Sephardi liturgy), there are three of these. The first is
for a deceased parent. If the parent is a father, its words are:

> May God remember the soul of my father and teacher,
> _____ the son of _____, who has gone to
> another world, wherefore I have donated charity in his
> name. And as his wage may his soul be bound in the
> bond of life with the souls of Abraham, Isaac, and Jacob,
> Sarah, Rebecca, Rachel, and Leah, and of all the righ-
> teous men and women in paradise, and say: amen.

The prayer for a mother is the same except for gender
changes. The idea that charitable donations made in the
name of the dead can, like reciting the kaddish, assist
their souls to enter paradise is first found in the ninth-
century Midrash Tanhuma, which refers to a practice of
"mentioning the dead on Yom Kippur and giving charity
on their behalf . . . so that they may bathe in rivers of balsam, milk, honey, and oil, and eat from the Tree of Life
that stands planted among the righteous with its boughs
hanging over them, and live forever." Since the *yizkor,* unlike the kaddish, can traditionally be recited by either sex,
the days on which it is said were ones when synagogues
were crowded with women who did not normally attend
services at other times. In effect, it *was* the woman's kaddish, as is attested by its mention of the four biblical ma-
triarchs, who do not appear alongside the three patriarchs
in other old prayers.

The second *yizkor* prayer includes family members the kaddish is not said for, such as grandparents, uncles, and aunts. The third begins: "May God remember the souls of all my male and female relatives, both on my father's side and on my mother's side, who were killed, murdered, slaughtered, burned, drowned, and suffocated for the sanctification of the Name."

"Sanctification of the Name [of God]"—*kiddush ha-shem*—is the Hebrew term for martyrdom, and this *yizkor* is probably closest to the original one, which was apparently composed in memory of the thousands of Jews killed by rampaging Crusaders in the Rhineland in 1096. Another prayer connected to the same event, *av ha-rahamim*, "Father of Mercy," is said every Sabbath at the same point in the service and joined to the *yizkor* when the latter is recited. After the members of the congregation silently recite the versions of the *yizkor* that are appropriate for them, the *el maley rahamim* is sung by the cantor.

Customarily, those having no one for whom to say the *yizkor* leave the synagogue while it is said. This naturally includes a high percentage of children. I can remember the mixture of relief and apprehension I felt as a child as we filed out. Although we welcomed the release from the tedium of the long holiday service to joke or play outside, with it went the knowledge that what was about to occur was too grim or frightening for us to behold. In a short story set in a nineteenth-century Polish shtetl, the Hebrew writer David Frischmann recounts his own childhood memory of the *yizkor*:

> Outside the synagogue stood a merry crowd, making a commotion, while the congregation within was enveloped

by a pall from front to back. A fear of God, a dark, holy dread, filled the house of worship. Slowly, the words [of the *yizkor* prayer] grazed the lips of the worshipers; the many candles whispered thinly and shadows danced on the walls. . . . Was it true that the souls of the dead assembled in the synagogue to hear themselves remembered? I stole a look through a crack in the door: perhaps I would recognize one of them.

When we filed back in, some of the faces that met our curious glances were red-eyed and tear-stained. I never made the connection between them and the destruction of European Jewry that had taken place only a few years previously. Growing up in America in the 1940s and '50s, one had less awareness of the Holocaust than Jewish children have now. We knew of it, of course, but it wasn't a subject that was talked about, certainly not in our presence, much less studied in schools. The shock of it was still too great for it to be spoken of in anything but hushed tones.

And yet many of those who had remained for the *yizkor* had lost family in the Holocaust. When they prayed for those "killed, murdered, slaughtered, burned, drowned, and suffocated for the sanctification of the Name," they weren't thinking of the Crusades. They were thinking of known names and faces, pictures they had seen in photograph albums, mail addressed in spiky handwritings beneath postage stamps from Poland, Lithuania, Latvia, Estonia, Rumania, Hungary, Germany. These were years in which many first- or second-generation American Jews still had contact with relatives in Europe.

"The lachrymose theory of Jewish history," the historian Salo Baron termed an undue emphasis on episodes of Jewish persecution. *Of course*: this history is more than a chronicle of mistreatment by others. Yet what shall we say about a people which, six million of its sons and daughters exterminated within a few years, has no need to compose a new prayer for them because a perfectly adequate one already exists? (Adequate? Prophetic! Who suffocated Jews at the time of the Crusades? Who knew then about Zyklon B?) Even the "Yizkor books," the commemorative volumes for the Jewish communities wiped out in World War II, have their precedent in the medieval *Memorbuchen* for Jewish victims of Christian violence. There are over a thousand of these, documenting pre-Holocaust life in places few of us have heard of: Amshinov, Andrychow, Apt, Baligrod, Bransk, Frampol, Glusk, Makow-Mazowiecki, Radashkovichy, Wislowiec, Zolochiv, Zychlin. They tell us who lived there, what they worked at, how they amused themselves, where they prayed, studied, played, congregated, and did business, the rivers they swam in, the woods they walked in, the names of their memorable characters and prominent citizens, their organizations, schools, charities, athletic associations, drama clubs, and political movements, their Orthodox, ultra-Orthodox, Zionists, Communists, and Bundists. They pool the memories of the survivors.

And yet what is all this in the end but a mere drop in a vast sea of oblivion? We can pray that the dead be granted eternal life—and we can try to grant it to them ourselves by remembering them. But how little we do remember and how little of that will be remembered by those who come after us. Who will read all the Yizkor books? And they, at least, preserve the names of those mentioned in them. Though many times the number of Jews who died in the Holocaust died ordinary deaths in the centuries before it, their names are now gone even from their tombstones, nearly all of which have been plowed under, carted away, erased by wind and rain, or overrun by the trees and bushes they stand among, half-buried in leaves like rocks on a forest floor.

This is hardly a uniquely Jewish fate. We let ourselves be comforted that the dead will live on in us while ignoring the discomforting truth that we, too, will not live on for very long. We strive to survive in memory by the name of a grandchild, an epithet on a tombstone, a donor's plaque, a book, a work of art, a pyramid or monumental sculpture, and time smiles and goes about its work. *And on the pedestal these words appear: "My name is Ozymandias, king of kings: Look on my works, ye Mighty, and despair!" Nothing beside remains.*

I sometimes ask myself: suppose I were thinking of writing a book that I would want to outlive me more than anything else that I have written—and suppose that someone with the power to make this happen offered to do so on the condition that my name not appear on it, so that no one would know I was its author. Would I still write it?

Possibly, I would. There is a joy in creation that has nothing to do with the craving to be remembered. But that craving is powerful. It's what makes the boy with the penknife carve his initials on the tree trunk, the traveler in the desert scratch his name on the rock. *I was here! This is who I was! This is what I saw! Don't forget me!* And we forget.

꽃

We forget. This was the point made by a poetic *yizkor* appearing in a book published in 1947 in what was still, scant months before the declaration of the state of Israel, the period of the British Mandate. A prayer for Holocaust refugees and survivors who had died at sea while trying to evade enforcement of the British ban on Jewish immigration to Palestine, it read in part:

> May God remember! . . . May He remember storm-tossed ships in wild seas ringed by towering waves, in their holds the broken of heart and crushed of spirit, one from a family and two from a town, fleers from doom who longed to shed their tears on the mountains of Zion. . . . May God remember! For we, who remember not the days of old, remember not the latter days, either, and what is our memory worth?

This *yizkor* had a background. In March 1920, the tiny Jewish agricultural commune of Tel Hai in the upper Galilee was overrun by hostile Bedouin and eight of its defenders were killed, among them Yosef Trumpeldor, already a legend for his decorated heroism in the 1905 Russo-Japanese War. At a memorial gathering for the eight in Tel Aviv, the Labor Zionist leader and intellectual Berl Katznelson gave the eulogy. In it was this *yizkor* written by him for the occasion:

> May the people of Israel remember the pure souls of its sons and daughters Shneur Shapushnik, Aharon Sher, Dvora Drachler, Binyamin Munter, Ze'ev Sharf, Sarah Chizik, Ya'akov Toker, and Yosef Trumpeldor. Brave and

loyal, they followed the plow and gave their lives for the honor and the soil of Israel. May all Israel remember and be blessed in its progeny, and may it mourn the glory of youth, the grace of courage, the holiness of will, and the dedication of spirit that perished in grievous battle. May our mourning know no rest, consolation, or end until the day when Israel redeems its pillaged land.

Katznelson's *yizkor* was a signal moment in the project of appropriating Jewish religious tradition for secular Zionism. No longer was God asked to remember the people of Israel. From now on, the people of Israel would remember its own.

This formulation struck roots in the Jewish community of Palestine and was widely invoked for Jews killed in the Arab disturbances of 1921 and 1929, the Arab revolt of 1936–39, and the anti-British struggle at the end of World War II. The 1947 *yizkor* was a religious Zionist protest against it. No longer ask God to remember? Who else *can* remember?

Since then, secular and religious *yizkor*s have contended with each other. After the establishment of the state of Israel, a reworked version of Katznelson's *yizkor* was adopted by the Israeli government and army and used at official ceremonies, such as those held on Yom Hazikaron, the country's Day of Remembrance for its fallen soldiers that directly precedes the celebrations of Independence Day. Amended several times to make it more inclusive, it now rather unwieldily reads:

May the people of Israel remember its brave and loyal sons and daughters, the soldiers of the Israel Defense Force; the fighters in the Jewish underground and in all the units that took part in the nation's battles; the

members of the intelligence community, defense depart-
ment, police force, and prison service who gave their
lives in the war for the rebirth of Israel; and all those
killed, whether in Israel or abroad, by the murderers
of terrorist organizations. May Israel remember and be
blessed in its progeny and mourn for the glory of youth,
and the grace of courage, and the holiness of will, and
the dedication of spirit of those who perished in grievous battle. May the victorious dead of the campaigns of
Israel be sealed in the hearts of Israel for all generations.

In Israeli religious circles, on the other hand, the traditional *yizkor* has continued to be said on such occasions,
and in deference to religious sensibilities it is also recited
in Yom Hazikaron's opening ceremony at Jerusalem's
Western Wall. In 2011, religious pressure led to the ap-
pointment of a military committee to consider adopting
it everywhere. Faced with strong secular resistance, the
committee voted to retain the status quo.

Yom Hazikaron is probably the closest thing to a sacred
secular day to exist in today's world. It begins at sunset, as
days do in the Jewish religious calendar. Much of our town
attends the ceremony, which is held out of doors. On a late
April or early May evening, it is already dark and chilly
when we congregate. In our sweaters and jackets, we take
our seats in long rows of plastic chairs; the waves and hel-
los are restrained, solemn. A flag flutters on its pole. At
eight o'clock a siren goes off, as it does at that exact moment all over the country. All stand for a minute of silence.
Then the flag is lowered to half-mast while an army bugler
sounds a retreat, *yizkor* is said, and a cantor sings *el maley
rahamim.*

The program that follows hasn't changed much since I first witnessed it. There are brief speeches by the mayor and town rabbi. A sad musical piece is played on a flute or recorder. A choir sings a wistful Hebrew song. Someone reads a poem about loss and its symbols: the empty room that never will be returned to, the changing of the seasons, the goodbye that turns out to be the last. Someone reads a pledge to the dead: *As your deaths have made our lives possible, so may our lives be worthy of your deaths.* Another musical piece, song, or poem. A passage from the Bible—perhaps Isaiah's prophecy of swords beaten into plow-shares. The list of the town's fallen is read aloud: it is longer than it used to be. All rise for Hatikvah, the national anthem whose name means "The Hope." The announcer proclaims, "The ceremony of the Day of Remembrance is over."

It's not always in that order and it's a bit different each time, but there are no surprises. One does not want to be surprised by a ritual. Rituals change nothing. They come to confirm. However grown, Israel is still a small country. When the siren sounds, everyone knows that everyone else has someone to focus on, a son, daughter, father, mother, brother, sister, neighbor, or friend. For many, it's more than one person. Once a year we gather to honor, not only the dead, but the pact sealed by their blood among the living.

The next morning there is a siren again. This time there are no public assemblies. All simply halt where they are, hands at their sides; no one moves until the siren's blast is over. The man walking to the bus stop, the woman pushing a baby carriage, the worker unloading cartons from a truck, the saleslady at her counter, the lawyers meeting in their office, the pupils in their classroom, the drivers pulling off the road to get out of their cars, the writer at his desk: each of them is encased in a frozen bubble. What would it look like, one wonders, through a telescope in space? A nation-wide children's game? A singular stoppage of time, like the time that has stopped for the dead in their graves?

For some, the rest of the day, if not spent watching tele-vision or listening to the radio, over which memorial pro-grams are broadcast nonstop, has no more special events. Others go to cemeteries, in which military ceremonies are held in the sections for the war dead, visit the families of fallen friends, or get together to reminisce about old battles and comrades killed in them. A minute's walk from our house, visible from a bedroom window, is a memorial for a dead soldier. A Jewish boy from ex-Yugoslavia who came to Israel by himself and was killed in a military action in Gaza, he had no family in this country. He did, though, have a girlfriend in our town. For several years she pes-tered its authorities until they agreed to donate a small plot of publicly owned land at the end of our street, after which she raised the money for a stone monument. In shape, it is suggestive of a Star of David. It has an inscription; a flag from which, standing at our window, we can tell which way the wind is blowing; and a bench beneath a hand-some olive tree that passersby and dog walkers sometimes sit on. Now and then, groups of soldiers are brought to it; their guide tells them its story while their eyes wander into the hills of the Carmel. Each Day of Remembrance, the dead boy's friends meet by its lowered flag. What they talk about, I don't know.

Nighttime. A room. The whisper I hear is my son's.
"Here I am. . . . My boys on the hill? . . . I'll be there."
It's still dark when he shoulders his pack and his gun.
And I think: God hasn't pledged he'll be spared.

So begins a poem by the Israeli sculptor and poet Dudi Ben-Ami. Even if its title were not "The Binding of Abraham," the literate Hebrew reader would know that the point of reference for its description of a young officer waked while on leave by an order to rejoin his troops is the biblical story of the binding of Isaac. "Here I am," *hineni,* archaic-sounding in today's Hebrew, is Abraham's response when God calls his name in Chapter 22 of Genesis. My translation's "on the hill," the poem's *al ehad he-harim,* echoes the Bible's "Take now your son, your only son Isaac, whom you love . . . and offer him there for a burnt offering on one of the hills that I will tell you of." The narrative in Genesis has its "boys," its *ne'arim,* too, Abraham's two young servants who accompany him and Isaac to Mount Moriah.

Few stories in the Bible speak so painfully to Jewish experience. When Jews in the Rhineland killed their children to keep them from falling into Crusader hands and being murdered or baptized, the *akeydah,* as the binding of Isaac is called in Hebrew, was repeatedly invoked by them. In the literature of a Jewish state that by now has sent four successive generations of its youth into battle, often to die or be maimed, the *akeydah* is frequently alluded to, too—but with a difference. In Jewish tradition, Abraham merits unstinting praise for being prepared to sacrifice the son he loves for the God he serves. Modern readers have a hard time with this. Wouldn't it have been more heroic of Abraham, they ask, to refuse God's command and say "No! Not even You are worth my son's death!"? And many Israelis, as patriotic as they may be, wonder at times whether they shouldn't say this to their country, too. They wonder—and send their sons off with their packs and guns. They know that were they to leave Israel before a son reached draft age, or use their connections, in a country in which personal ties count for much, to have the army assign him to a noncombat position, someone else's son would have to risk death in his place.

Unless the speaker indicates otherwise, the Hebrew word *shkhol,* whose dictionary meaning is "bereavement," specifically refers in contemporary Israeli speech to the loss of a child, most commonly, a young soldier. When Yitzhak Rabin, in his remarks on the White House lawn at the signing of the 1993 Oslo Agreement, said of his coun- trymen, "We come from a land in which parents bury their children," he was not exaggerating for rhetorical purposes. Yet when I, who have lived in this land for the better part of my life, try to imagine burying a child of my own, I cannot. I do not believe I could emerge emotionally intact from such an experience; I can only think of being broken beyond repair. This is what one commonly hears from the bereaved parents interviewed on television and radio on Yom Hazikaron. "You never get over it." "It just gets worse from year to year."

The child who buries his parents does not constantly think from year to year: *If my father were alive, he might be doing this now. This year, my mother would have been old enough for that.* But the parents who bury their children are tormented by such thoughts. They live two lives: their own and the life their child never had. They may want to live the child's more. The Israeli novelist David Grossman, whose son was killed commanding a tank in the 2006 war in Lebanon, has written a work called *Falling Out of Time* that is a modern version of the ancient epic of *Gilgamesh*. Setting out for a place that he refers to only as "There" in order to find the son he has lost, the book's nameless hero gathers around him on his journey a party of bereaved parents like himself, each looking for a dead child. "There" is a destination they never reach, but as is true of many journeys, what matters is what happens along the way. At one point, the main character,

walking, still walking,
not asleep and
not awake, walking
and emptying
of all that is me,

declares:

Look at me, son:
I no longer am.
I'm just the living matrix
that calls to you to come
and be through me—
to come alive, if only for a moment,
and once more belong
to reality. . . .
My blood's your blood,
my muscles, too, are yours. Come,
be,

stretch out your arms
to the world's far end,
laugh from my throat, roar, bray,
throw away
all inhibition.
For this brief moment all is possible,
all is *yes*.
Love, burn, covet,
screw—
my starved five senses
stand at your command
like five horses champing at the bit,
stamping, stamping,
set to race
to the infinity of you.

But this is fantasy. One cannot bequeath one's body
to a dead child. Would *shkhol* be easier to bear if Israelis
felt differently about their country than so many of them
have come to do—if it did not seem to them doomed to
unending conflict with its neighbors and bitter dissension
among its citizens? Losing a child in a nation's war can
be more meaningful than losing a child to cancer or in an
automobile accident—provided one believes, as Grossman
did not, that the war served a purpose. The more doubts
Israelis have come to have about the battles their country fights, the more they have treated death in them as
if it *were* a terrible accident. The stoic acceptance of sacrifice they once prided themselves on has given way to
a media-driven preoccupation with grief. Devastated parents, teary friends, weeping funerals: all are now grist for
the evening news.

Our enemies see this and rejoice twice: once at the sorrow they have caused us and once at our weakness in showing it. A people so afraid of death, they crow, will never fight to the end. We retort that fear of death is no weakness; that whoever loves life bewails its loss; that a culture of suicide bombers and *shahid*s will lose its will to live before we do. Although I tend to believe this is so, I sometimes wish we gave our enemies less satisfaction. Why let them witness our anguish?

Ben-Ami's poem concludes:

> Who'll return? Lord, lay not your hand.
> He'll go first, my son, at the head.
> Where's the end?
> The lamb is burned whole once again.
> On the altar,
> Abraham's people lies bound.

One morning while I was writing this book, I went to the offices of our town's religious council to inquire about purchasing burial plots for my wife and me. This was something we had put off doing for years. Although neither of us doubted our mortality, acquiring graves had seemed an untimely concession to it. Besides, they cost money and we had always been short of that. Israel's ministry of religion guarantees everyone a free burial, but this doesn't come with the prerogative of choosing where or next to whom you will be buried. If you're at all picky, you have to pay for your preferences.

And what did we need graves for, anyway? We had our own burial cave, even if no one had been in it since the teenage son of some people we knew fell seriously ill with tick fever caught while exploring it.

Indeed, we might have put it off even longer had not my wife stopped in the street one day to chat with Herzl—not Herzl the Zionist, but Herzl the gardener who had once worked for our neighbors and was now employed by the local hevra kadisha. Between one thing and another, he informed her that our local cemetery was filling up quickly. If we didn't want to be shunted off somewhere else when we died, we had better purchase plots now.

A man at the religious council sat me down at a desk and consulted his computer. Then he wrote something on a slip of paper and handed it to me. "Here," he said. "What's left is in the bottom section of the new cemetery. We're up to Row 6. Plots 1 to 21 are doubles. Twenty-two to 50 are singles. One to 9 and 12 to 35 are still available."

"Doubles?" I asked.

"That's one of you above the other. Whoever dies first, goes below."

The prices were on the slip of paper. We could pay in four monthly installments.

We went the next day to have a look. The bottom section of the new cemetery has its own gate, but we entered at the main gate and walked through the old cemetery first. It's nice there. The graves are laid out in short, intimate rows, some grouped in irregular clusters where families or friends lie together. Many of the headstones have been stroked and fingered by time; tall cypress trees grow over them. Some bear the names of people whose biers we've walked behind along the main street from the synagogue in the town square. Once this was the common practice. Today it's done rarely, mostly for the town's old families, and has something of the aspect of a state funeral.

The old families are buried in the old cemetery. As we descended to the new one, the rows of graves grew longer and straighter, the spaces between them narrower. The bottom section was the stingiest; there wasn't a tree or even room for one. Though mostly unoccupied, it had been ruled off in its entirety into rectangular plots. It was as if Death were saying, "Take your time if you wish, but I'm ready." As if it said, "Yes, I'm hungry, but I'm patient. I know I always get fed in the end."

Row 6 was bare except for two headstones. Plot 50 was at the near end. Close to the gate, it abutted a concrete walk that separated the new cemetery's bottom section from the one above it. Plot 1 was at the far end, bordered by an iron fence beyond which were the houses of the town. We walked to it along an aisle barely wide enough for one of us and stood looking down at it. "I like the idea of our being in one grave," I said to my wife. "If I die first, I'll warm the bed for you."

She threw me a sharp look. She disapproves of black humor. "I like it, too," she said. "But there's no room here for anyone to stand. What will people do at our funerals? They'll have to walk in single file just to get here."

She's always thinking of others. I'd be happy to let the people at my funeral fend for themselves. "Let's go look at the other end," she said.

We walked back to it. "This is better," my wife said. "It's right off the walk. There's room to gather. We'll just have to be buried side by side."

"We'll hold hands," I said. "But 36 to 50 are taken."

We stood glumly contemplating the alternatives. "We should have bought something in the old cemetery years ago," said my wife.

"Well, we didn't," I said. "But I have an idea. Let's wait for Row 6 to fill up. Then we can ask for the front graves in Row 7."

"Suppose someone asks for them before us."

"We'll talk to Herzl," I said. "He has pull. He'll get the religious council to put them aside for us."

That's what we decided to do. I left the cemetery with a feeling of relief. We had put off buying graves once again.

❧

"Wake up."

My wife stirs.

"The buses for Jerusalem are here."

"I'm sleeping."

"They've already called rows 1 and 2."

"What time is it?"

"How would I know what time it is? I don't know what century it is."

"Wake me at eight."

"But the buses are here."

"No, nine."

This *is* absurd, I think. We're being resurrected and it's totally, totally absurd.

❧

"Look at the light on the Carmel."

"It's magnificent."

"I love this time of day. All the birds are flying home."

"If we were ancient Greeks, we'd think those gulls were an augury."

"They're heading for the sea."

"Listen to the bulbul. That's its good-night song."

"Can you see it?"

"No. It's in that tree somewhere."

"There it goes!"

"And there's the other one."

"They're always together."

"They marry for life."

"Like us. What do you think happens when one dies?"

"You mean does the other find someone else?"

"Yes."

"I don't think so. It probably folds its wings and dies too."

"That's what I'd want to do if you died."

"Me too. But then I'd fly away and find you."

"Where?"

"In the country of the dead."

"I wish you wouldn't talk like that."

"Why?"

"Because it scares me. That's why I never wanted you to write a book about death."

"You think it's had a morbid effect on me?"

"I'd rather you thought about life."

"But how can a love like ours simply disappear? Doesn't it have to go on existing *somewhere*?"

"I don't think about it."

"I do."

"Let's talk about something else."

For the most part, contemporary Judaism has preferred to talk about something else, too. Reading its most prominent thinkers, one notes the near-total absence of the afterlife in their works. This is true not only of the non-Orthodox. I take down from my bookshelves the writings of some of the leading Orthodox or neo-Orthodox theologians of our times: Rosenzweig, Soloveitchik, Heschel, Levinas, Leibowitz, Berkovits, Fackenheim. I turn their pages. If they have indexes, I look for the words "immortality," "after-life," "world-to-come." There's hardly anything. Even Franz Rosenzweig, who thought all religion, not just its primitive prototype, began with man's "quivering with terror" before the specter of death, has no more to say about Judaism's promises of immortality than that they are "quite beyond the imagination." And this, though countless Jewish minds before him imagined the afterlife profusely and regarded a belief in it, in one form or another, to be a prerequisite of Jewish faith.

Such would seem to be the attitude of a high propor-tion of rank-and-file Orthodox Jews as well, or at least of those who would add "Modern" to the "Orthodox." While there is a lively discussion in the Modern Orthodox world as to exactly when, halakhically speaking, death occurs and what the bioethical implications of this are, there is mostly silence about what, if anything, happens to the dead *after* dying. Not long ago, I asked someone belong-ing to one of the strongest and best-educated Modern

Orthodox communities in the United States whether he thought a belief in the world-to-come played an important role in the religion of its members. He answered: "It certainly doesn't play a role in *my* religion. I suppose it might in some people's, but I wouldn't know who they were, because it's not something that comes up in conversation. I've never encountered it as a serious proposition." His experience is confirmed by a series of interviews about the afterlife conducted with some of her traditionally observant acquaintances by the American Orthodox writer and activist Blu Greenberg. Although she found, Greenberg writes, "a range of belief and disbelief," even the belief-end of the spectrum showed no more than "a very tenuous acknowledgment of the impact of such concepts on one's actions in the present life"—which is to say, the whole question didn't matter much to anyone. Others besides her, Greenberg observes, have reached similar conclusions.

When one considers that today's Orthodox Jews are as punctilious in their ritual practice as most observant Jews have been in the past, it's striking how easily they have sloughed off assumptions about the world-to-come held to be basic to Judaism for millennia. While Modern Orthodoxy generally operates with a kind of split vision that keeps one eye on the truths of science and the other on the dogmas of religion, the dogma of an afterlife has been pushed to the margins. Is this because the old biblical view of death as for all intents and purposes final is perceived to be a sufficient underpinning when the superstructure built on it by later generations no longer seems intellectually tenable? Does it perhaps even reflect a sense of returning to a *truer* Judaism? Although this is not something that anyone loyal to rabbinic tradition would care to acknowledge, it still might be intuitively felt.

Yet not everyone is for changing the subject when it comes to the world-to-come. There is by now a considerable body of writing that argues against contemporary Judaism's neglect of the afterlife and for a return to a serious consideration of it. Like many developments in Jewish thought, this one can be traced to non-Jewish influences—specifically, to the "New Ageism" of the late twentieth century and the work of thanatologists like Elizabeth Kűbler-Ross, Raymond Moody, Ian Stevenson, Pim van Lommel, and others, who claim to have found empirical evidence for a hereafter. The fact that many of these figures have been medical doctors or psychiatrists has lent their research a measure of credibility.

There's no need to read a great deal of it, because it's highly repetitive. Over and over one encounters in it case studies of critically ill patients or accident victims who recall, upon recovering from near or clinical death, the same or many of the same things: leaving their bodies and observing them and the events taking place around them from a vantage point outside them; seeing their lives pass before them in a summarizing review; entering a tunnel or crossing a bridge at the end of which is a field of brilliant light; being welcomed there by dead family members, old friends, or celestial guides; being led by these figures through scenes of pastoral beauty while experiencing feelings of joy, ecstasy, and oneness with the universe; being told, despite their desire to remain in so blissful a place, that their time has not yet come and that they must return to their earthly bodies and duties; and doing so with regret but with a new awareness, emancipated from the fear of death, of the spiritual nature of all things. The very similarity of such experiences has been taken to be proof of their veracity, there being no other reasonable explanation, it is claimed, for their being had by so many people of different backgrounds, educational levels, and religious beliefs or the lack of them.

There have been attempts to relate such material to the traditional concepts of Judaism. In his book *Jewish Views of the Afterlife*, for example, the scholar and psychotherapist Simcha Paull Raphaell points out that the commonly reported "life review" has close parallels in rabbinic sources, as in this passage from the tractate of Ta'anit:

> When a person goes to his eternal home, all his deeds take leave of him. "Such-and-such," he is told, "was done by you in such-and-such a place on such-and-such a day"—and when he says, "Yes," he is told "Sign!" and he signs.

At other times, Raphaell bends or allegorizes, as when the bright radiance encountered in many near-death experiences is equated by him with the *nehar di-nur*, the "river of fire" of the Jewish world-to-come, even though this river is described in most Jewish sources as painfully purging, not joyfully illuminating. Choosing to translate the Aramaic word *nur*, "fire," as "light," Raphaell writes:

> Individuals who have practiced a meditative discipline and become familiar with altered states of consciousness may recognize . . . the River of Light as the inner luminosity of the soul and receptively bask in its radiance. Those who have not acquired a familiarity with the higher experiential realities of consciousness may actually be

completely unaware and unconscious during this early phase of the postmortem journey. Or perhaps the intensity of the River of Light may evoke fear and fright.

Such emotions, Raphaell holds, are responses to purely subjective factors. Kűbler-Ross, Moody, et al. record few cases of near-death anguish or torment. Nearly all their informants testify to feelings of peace, serenity, and love (the ubiquitous, all-pervasive cosmic existence of which is a central motif in the New Age thanatology), and Raphaell accordingly proposes that any suffering in the afterlife is not God's punishment but the unenlightened soul's misperception of God's glory. Gehenna, he writes,

> provides a concentrated opportunity to encounter the dark and dishonorable, unresolved negative emotions. . . . Gehenna is not a locale so much as a state of consciousness, an experiential realm reflecting one's own emotional state. . . . [D]escriptions of the torments of Gehenna, which abound in rabbinic and medieval Midrash and Kabbalah, are to be seen as symbolic and not literal. Like the *bardo* visions of the *Tibetan Book of the Dead* and Christian images of hell, they describe in allegory and metaphoric language different aspects of the process of purgation and emotional purification.

Raphaell and others refer frequently to the *Tibetan Book of the Dead,* between which and Jewish tradition they draw numerous parallels. This has the effect of both validating and vitiating the tradition's claims to knowledge of the afterlife, since by anchoring these in Buddhism, a religion, unlike Christianity and Islam, historically unconnected to Judaism, it affirms their essential truth while denying their uniquenesss. But such is the ecumenical wisdom of our times, for which all religions reflect the same core human experience and can serve as equally useful vehicles for exploring it.

I have no firm opinion of the life-after-deathers. Those of them I have read a bit of, such as Kűbler-Ross, Moody, and the psychiatrist Brian Weiss, who has sought to document the existence of former lives, do not strike me as quacks or charlatans. Their work is sincere. One can challenge its methodology and data, as its would-be debunkers have done. One can offer alternative explanations of the cases that pass scrutiny, based on the hypothesis that the brain, on the verge of dying, or while being reactivated during recovery, hallucinates, has distorted spatial and temporal perceptions, and processes memories in an accelerated, nonlinear fashion, all in conformity with prior notions about death that have been culturally implanted in it. But though such explanations, even if unable to account for everything, make a good deal of sense, I feel no more compelled to accept them in the name of a hard-edged materialism than to reject them in the name of a more crumbly-edged spiritualism. I muse about the matter, as my wife wishes I wouldn't, and turn my thoughts to other things, as she wishes I would.

And *this,* I must say, is strange. I am an inmate, after all, in a prison. Every day the guards come, select some of my fellow prisoners, and march them off to execution. When I look for a logic in their selection, I cannot find any; men, women, and children are taken in seemingly arbitrary fashion. Still, each group includes a disproportionate number of elderly people like myself. Day by day, more and more of us are marched away, and day by day, I know that my chances of being in the next batch are greater. This frightens me. I don't sleep well. I lie awake at night waiting for the footsteps of the guards.

But the steps of the person now slipping into my cell are not a guard's. They belong to a prisoner who was taken to be shot and has returned with an incredible story. Lined up against a wall and told to say his prayers, he fainted and slumped to the ground—and when he opened his eyes he saw that a door in the wall had opened and all were being invited to step through it into a world of green valleys and flowing streams where they were joyfully welcomed by the prisoners who had gone before them. He himself, however, was stopped at this door and told to return to his prison cell, because his name on the list of those taken that day was a mistake. The execution, he informs us, is a sham. It is simply a pedagogical trick played on us by our jailers to make us more appreciative of the world beyond the door.

Should I believe him? Yet isn't it likely that he dreamed all this after passing out and being dragged away from the wall while the other prisoners were in fact shot and killed? My life literally depends on the answer. I listen to him a while longer, lose interest in what he is saying, and ask the man on the cot next to mine if he would care for a game of chess.

Why do the good tidings from the beyond not grip me more? Even if it is reasonable to assume that they're only a neurological malfunction of the temporal lobe or prefrontal cortex, don't they still offer a ray of hope that death might not be the end of me? Shouldn't I clutch at this hope as a man does at a lifeline, however frail, that's been thrown him?

And perhaps I would if only those returned from the frontier of death had seen and felt something noteworthy there—something more striking than the same undiffer-entiated golden light, beautiful clouds, gardens of flowers, and smiling beings in white robes, something less uni-formly misty than "total love," "a deepest sense of peace and truth," and "being one with the Creator."

Something more like this morning.

When I stepped out this morning to see if the paper had been delivered, the world was all blacks and grays. It had rained during the night and the needles of the pine trees by the driveway brushed cold drops across my face. From nearby came the first sound of the day.

Chuk chuk. It was a bulbul. "I'm up," it announced. *Chuk chuk chuk.* "Where are you?"

Chuk chuk chuk. "Here I am." The answer came from somewhere off to my left.

The bulbul near me switched to a snatch of song. *Kwee tooey tooey, kwee tooey tooey,* it sang.

Kwee tooey tooey, kwee tooey tooey, the second bulbul sang back.

The first bulbul added a note. *Kwee tooey tooey kwee, kwee tooey tooey kwee.* Bulbuls are fine singers. I've never been able to count how many musical phrases they know. They vary them so constantly that they seem endless.

This went unanswered. After a while, the first bulbul repeated it.

Now came the reply, faint and further away. *Kwee tooey tooey kwee, kwee tooey tooey kwee.*

Chuk chuk chuk chuk chuk, the first bulbul said loudly.

I stood listening. How many mornings like this had they exchanged the same glad greetings, asked the same anxious questions, given the same soothing assurances? "Are you still there?" "No, now I'm here." "Don't go too far without me." "You know I'd never do that."

The paper hadn't come yet.

When I went to look for it again a half-hour later, the world was on fire. Scarlet flames streaked the eastern sky. A girder of black at their base was barred with red like a bed of hot coals. Recessed within it, like a mountain lake at the bottom of a burning forest, shone a serene pocket of blue. The fire raged and slowly burned itself out. The scarlet flames turned vermilion, then faded to airy oranges and pinks while the coals went a dull gray. And then, all at once, as if plunged into the bath of blue from the anvil it had been hammered out on, a glistening disk cleared the horizon.

It was just the birth of another day on earth, but if heaven has anything to match it with, the news has yet to be brought back.

There is a long midrash about the death of Moses. In the Bible, this takes place as the people of Israel are about to cross the Jordan to possess the land promised them—a promise that Moses, in punishment for a misdeed in the desert, has been told by God he will not live to see fulfilled. Now, at the age of one-hundred-twenty, he is instructed to ascend Mount Nebo and view the land from afar before he dies.

In the midrash, Moses refuses to accept God's decree. Having successfully prayed many times for mercy for the stiff-necked Israelites, he is confident of his ability to plead his own cause. Indeed, so powerful are his prayers, cutting and slashing through all obstacles, that God, afraid He might be moved by them, orders His angels to shut and bolt the gates of heaven against them.

The path of prayer blocked, Moses takes to arguing. The Torah says, "Thou shalt not oppress a hired hand; at the end of the day thou shalt give him his wages." Where are his wages, he asks, for having led the Israelites in the desert for forty years? He has been exploited like an unpaid laborer.

God seeks to reason with him. "If I don't take your life in this world," He explains, "how can I reward you with life in the next one?"

But it is life in this world that Moses wants. "Lord," he pleads, "if You will not let me enter the Land, let me live on as a beast of the fields that eats grass and drinks rainwater."

"Enough, Moses," God says.

"Master of the Universe!" Moses persists. "If not as a beast of the field, then as a bird that flies here and there, seeking its food each day and returning each night to its nest. I ask no more."

"Moses, enough!" God repeats.

Moses will not be silenced. "Master of the Universe! This face that looked on Yours on Mount Sinai—these legs that climbed its heights and trod the fog—these arms in which You placed Your Torah: are they all now to lick the dust?"

"So I have decreed and such is the way of the world," God replies. "Each generation has its teachers. Each has its providers. Each has its leaders. Until now, it was your lot to serve me. From now on, it's your pupil Joshua's."

"Master of the Universe!" Moses says. "If I must die to make way for Joshua, let me be his pupil instead."

"If that's your wish," God shrewdly replies, "you have my permission."

The next morning, Moses rises and goes to Joshua's tent for a Torah lesson. Although Joshua recoils at the presumption of teaching his revered teacher, God, the midrash tells us, passes "the reins of wisdom" from Moses to him and commands him to give the lesson, which Moses, to his dismay, cannot understand. Worse, asked afterward by his classmates to explain its subtleties, he is humiliated by having to admit he cannot. "Master of the Universe," he tells God, "I had wanted to live, but now You can have my life."

God has won. Loath, however, to put His beloved prophet in the hands of Samael, the Angel of Death, He tells the archangel Gabriel, "Go bring me Moses' soul." "Master of the Universe!" protests Gabriel. "How can I attend the death of a man who is the equal of all six hundred thousand Israelites who left Egypt?"

God then makes the same request of the archangel Michael, with whom Moses studied Torah every day. "How can I attend the death of the man whose tutor I was?" Michael demurs.

And so God has to ask Samael, who is happy to perform the chore. Strapping on his sword, he marches fiercely off to find Moses. Yet, encountering him, Samael is so awed by the sun-like radiance of Moses' visage that his knees buckle and he is left speechless.

"What are you doing here?" Moses asks.

"I've come to take your soul," stammers Samael.

"You can't have it," says Moses.

"But the souls of all the living are in my hands," Samael insists.

"I am the son of Amram who was born circumcised from my mother's womb," Moses tells him. "I spoke and walked the moment I was born. I performed miracles in Egypt and delivered six hundred thousand Israelites from bondage. I tore the Red Sea to pieces, and climbed the heavens to receive a Torah writ in fire, and lodged beneath God's seat of glory, and spoke with Him face to face. Who among the living can do such things? Be gone, you wretch! My soul isn't yours to take."

The Angel of Death reports to God that Moses refuses to surrender his soul to him. "Go back and take it," God orders him. Drawing his sword, Samael advances on Moses again. Moses brandishes his staff, on which is engraved God's sacred name, and gives Samael such a blow with it that he turns and flees.

"Moses," proclaims a heavenly voice, determined to put an end to the matter, "your day has come to die."

"Master of the Universe," Moses remonstrates, "don't You remember how You revealed Yourself to me in the burning bush, and how You told me to go to Pharaoh and make him let my people go, and how I did? Don't you remember the forty days and nights that I spent on Mount Sinai receiving the Torah? I beg you, don't hand me over to the Angel of Death."

"Don't be afraid," the voice proclaims. "I will attend to you myself."

Whereupon, the midrash relates, God descended from His highest heaven to take Moses' soul, accompanied by Gabriel, Michael, and Zagzagael. Michael made Moses' bed, Gabriel spread a fine linen garment at the head of it, Zagzagael spread another at its foot, and God said to Moses, "Shut your eyes."

Moses shut his eyes.

"Lay your hands upon your chest."

Moses laid his hands on his chest.

"Straighten your legs."

Moses straightened his legs.

God said to Moses' soul:

"My child, I have given you one-hundred-and-twenty years to be in Moses' body. Now depart from it."

"Master of the Universe," said Moses' soul. "I know that You are the Lord of all souls, and that the living and the dead are in Your hands, and that You created me and placed me in Moses' body for one-hundred-and-twenty years. But is there a holier body in the entire world? I love it and don't want to leave it."

"Come, waste no more time," God said. "I promise to bring you to the highest heaven and install you beneath My seat of glory with the cherubs and the seraphs."

"Master of the Universe," begged the soul, "please let me stay in Moses' body."

But God kissed Moses on the mouth and drew his soul from him with the kiss. And He wept and said, "Who will now rise up for me against the evildoers? Who will now stand up for me against the workers of iniquity?"

A remarkable midrash! From it comes the Hebrew expression *mitat neshikah,* "death by a kiss," signifying a painless death that involves no suffering, neither before nor at the moment of dying. But the kiss is God's, not death's.

Death was never eroticized by Judaism. No one dies in its arms like Shakespeare's Cleopatra, rejoicing in it "as a lover's pinch, which hurts and is desired." It always arrives with a sword.

Such a death is but one of the midrash's novel features. Even more startling is its description of a Moses who, though having reached the pinnacle of age and human achievement, is so desperate to stay alive that he would do so even as an animal. This is not the behavior of a great and wise prophet. It is that of a terrified man who, in Franz Rosenzweig's words, "roars Me! Me! Me!" while knowing that "his I would be but an It if he dies." In the frantic clutches of the will to live, writes Rosenzweig, man cries "his very I out with every cry that is still in his throat against Him from whom there is no appeal, from whom such unthinkable annihilation threatens."

Moses cries his I out. None of Judaism's consolations mean a thing to him. The rabbis' world-to-come with its all glories is not the slightest comfort—and this, in a rabbinical tale! But neither is he gathered to his people. He, who fashioned it, dies without it, with no one at his funeral, with no one even knowing where his grave is. He is as alone with God in death as he was on Mount Sinai.

And yet how quickly, confronted with the loss of his powers, he changes his mind and is ready to die!

This speed is a narrative device. In real life, it doesn't happen that way. But whether we think of the midrash as condensing into a moment the gradual lapse into social irrelevance of retirement and old age, the inexorable decay of the body, the slow mental deterioration of senility, or the more acute course of fatal illness, Moses' stunned realization of his decline is true to human experience. There is always that first terrible moment of awareness. One thinks of the consternation, caught by a camera, of the eighty-seven-year-old Toscanini, a man renowned for his musical memory, when forgetting the score during a performance of Wagner's *Tannhäuser.* He never conducted publicly again and died a few years later.

Most of us die too soon or too late. When a stock goes up, it's no time to sell. When it goes down, we should have sold already.

Most of us, of course, do not decide when our deaths will be. And even if it were more acceptable to do so, most of us would not want to make the decision, not only on moral or religious grounds, but because we wouldn't trust our own judgment. A stock drops, you sell, and it's back up.

There are days on which I want to live forever. There are days on which I'm glad I won't. And then the weather changes and again I want it never to end. And it's precisely then that I think, "It's good it's not in my hands."

On both kinds of days I marvel: *How did it go by so fast?* This must be a universal reaction to growing old. Everyone my age seems to have it. Yet not everyone prayed as a boy for another year of the life he was afraid he wouldn't have. Had I been guaranteed then that I would be given twenty years and not a day more, I would have felt boundlessly blessed. Twenty years were a fortune. Why would I possibly want more? And now sixty have passed as though in a dream and they haven't been nearly enough.

What is man, says the Yom Kippur prayer. *Like the jar that breaks, and the grass that withers, and the flower that fades, and the shadow that passes, and the cloud that melts, and the wind that blows, and the dust that is blown, and the dream that is gone.*

If life is a dream, what does that make death?

There was an envelope in today's mail. It came from the religious council. In it were two certificates. The one in my name said:

The above has purchased, for use after one-hundred-and-twenty, a grave site in the cemetery of Zichron Ya'akov.

Area	Section	Row	Number
A	6	7	45

The second certificate was for Number 46.

"After one-hundred-and-twenty" is another Hebrew and Yiddish expression connected to the story of Moses. It's a euphemistic way of saying of someone, "When he's dead and gone." "After one-hundred-and-twenty, she'll leave them her property." "The strongbox is to be opened after one-hundred-and-twenty."

So you might say we're all set.

But we're not, not at all.

Wouldn't it be nice if it could be with a kiss, though?

※

I would like to thank Neal Kozodoy, the editor of the Library of Jewish Ideas, for commissioning this book, waiting for it patiently, and reading and commenting on its drafts. Although I have worked extensively with Neal for—unbelievably enough—nearly half a century in his capacities as editor of *Commentary* and *Mosaic* magazines, this is his first involvement in a book of mine. My long association with him is an honor I am proud of.

My thanks also go to Fred Appel of Princeton University Press for his steady encouragement and support; to Isaac Pollak, leader of the Men's hevra kadisha of Congregation Kehilath Jeshurun of Manhattan, for generously sharing his time and knowledge with me; and to Jodi Beder, this book's copy editor, for her careful attention to it.

※

Many subjects have been touched on in these pages that readers may wish to pursue further. Here are some English books I've read that might prove helpful.

On concepts of the afterlife in antiquity: *Life after Death: A History of the Afterlife in the Religions of the West* by Alan F. Segal; *Paradise in Antiquity: Jewish and Christian Views*, edited by Markus Bockmuehl and Guy G. Stroumsa; and *Resurrection and the Restoration of Israel* by Jon D. Levenson.

For an overall survey of Jewish thinking about the hereafter: *Jewish Views of the Afterlife* by Simcha Paull Rafael.

On the history of the kaddish and associated issues of mourning: *Kaddish* by Leon Wieseltier.

On Jewish thought and custom related to death and dying in the late medieval and early modern period in Europe: *Crossing the Jabbok* by Sylvie Anne Goldberg (translated from French by Carol Cosman).

On such thought and custom in our own time: *When a Jew Dies* by Samuel C. Heilman; *The Jewish Mourner's Companion* by Zalman Goldstein; *The Spiritual Journey beyond Grief* by Maurice Lamm; and *Jewish Insights on Death and Mourning*, edited by Jack Riemer.

On the New Age thanatology and its critics: *On Life after Death* by Elisabeth Kűbler-Ross; *Reflections on Life after Life* by Raymond Moody; *Does the Soul Survive? A Jewish Journey to Belief in Afterlife, Past Lives and Living with a Purpose* by Elie Kaplan Spitz; and *Out-of-Body and Near-Death Experiences: Brain-State Phenomena or Glimpses of Immortality?* by Michael N. Marsh.

Apart from verses from the Bible, where I have relied on the King James Version while at times slightly amending it for my purposes, the translations in this book of all passages from the Talmud and Midrash, medieval Jewish authors, and Hasidic and modern Hebrew and Yiddish literature are my own with one exception: the text of Rabbi Yehoshua ben Levi's vision of paradise in Chapter 2, where I have used William G. Braude's translation in his English edition of Hayyim Nahman Bialik and Yehoshua Ravnitzky's *Book of Legends*. All translations of the Pseudepigrapha are taken from *The Old Testament Pseudepigrapha*, edited by James H. Charlesworth. The quotation from Franz Rosenzweig in Chapter 5 is from William W. Hallo's translation of Rosenzweig's *Star of Redemption*.

I did not originally intend this book to have reference notes. Despite the research that went into it, it is not a scholarly work and I did not want its readers to be distracted by the apparatus of scholarship. Yet when the manuscript was submitted for publication, the editors thought such notes would be useful to readers wishing to consult sources quoted from or cited by me, and I agreed to provide them on condition that no attention be called to them in the text itself. They appear below in order of the page on which the referenced citation or quotation is found.

4: "The days of our years are threescore years and ten": Psalms 90:10.
5: the two contending schools of early rabbinic Judaism: This dispute is treated of in the Talmudic tractate of Eruvin 13b.
5: *Eyn adam yotsey min ha'olam*: Kohelet Rabba 1:34.
6: "Truly, the light is sweet": Kohelet 11:7.
9: "When in your ship you have crossed": *Odyssey,* Book 10, ll. 505–15.

11: "dirt is their drink": *Epic of Gilgamesh*, Tablet 7, l. 979.

12: "the good receive a life free from toil": Pindar, *Second Olympian*, ll. 70–73.

13: "What man can live and never see death?": Psalms 89:49.

13: "Shall I ransom them": Hosea, 13:14.

13: "I shall go down in mourning": Genesis 37:35.

13: "whom, opening its mouth": Numbers 16:33.

13: "I will make the nations quake": Ezekiel 31:16–18.

13: "the maggot as your bed": Isaiah 14:11.

14: "Why did I not die at birth": Job 3:11, 17.

14: the witch of En-Dor: I Samuel 28.

14: "Do not turn to conjurers": Leviticus 19:31.

17: "See, I have set before you": Deuteronomy 30:15.

17: "In death there is no remembrance": Psalms 6:6.

17: the conjurers who "chirp and mutter": Isaiah 8:19.

17: "He who touches the dead body": Numbers 19:11–13.

17: "And your carcass shall be food": Deuteronomy 28:26.

18: The story of the "man of God" from Judah: I Kings 13.

19: The story of Ritzpa bat Aya: II Samuel 21. The story of the Gileadites: I Samuel 31.

20: like that bought by Abraham in Hebron: Genesis, Chapter 23.

21: the tractate of Bava Batra: Mishnah of Bava Batra 6:8.

22: "You shall not slash": Deuteronomy 14:1.

22–23: The story in the book of Kings of Elijah and the priests of the Baal: I Kings 7.

23: David's infant son: II Samuel 12.

23: "lay down with his fathers": II Kings 2:10

24–25: "All the commandments": Deuteronomy 8, 1–2, 19.

25: "Let his posterity be cut off": Psalms 109:13.

25: "That his name be not erased from Israel": Deuteronomy 25:6.

27: "For behold, I will create new heavens": Isaiah 65:17.

27: "For behold, the day is coming": Malachi 3:19, 23.

28: "visit the iniquity of the fathers upon the children": Exodus 20:5.

28: "no one shall say any more": Jeremiah 31: 28–29.

28: "The son shall not bear the iniquity of the father": Ezekiel 18: 17–20.

29: "The Lord giveth and the lord taketh": Job: 1:21.

29: "You know I am not guilty": Job 10:7.

30: "All is vanity": Kohelet 1:1.

30: "they blow to the south": Kohelet 1:6.

30: "I saw under the sun": Kohelet 3: 16–19.

31: In his *Republic*, Plato's Socrates: *The Republic*, Book 10.

31: said by the book of Genesis "to have walked with God": Genesis 5:24.

32: "And at that time shall Michael stand up": Daniel 12: 1–2.

32: A vision of the dry bones: Ezekiel 37.

34: The figure of the "Elect One" or "Anointed One": I Enoch 48.

34: "cries, wails, and screams of great pain": I Enoch 108:5.

34: "A generation of righteous ones shall arise": I Enoch 107:1.

35: "third heaven": Life of Adam and Eve 37:5.

36: "And they brought me up to the third heaven": II Enoch 8:1–8.

37: "whether it was in the body or out of it": II Corinthians 12:2.

37: "a great crowd in the likeness of men": Apocalypse of Abraham 15:16.

39: "Let your loins be girded": Luke 12:35–36.

39: "There be some of you standing here": Luke 9:27, Mark 9:1, Matthew 16:28.

39: from "the uttermost parts": Mark 13:27.

40: "every soul is immortal": Josephus, *The Jewish War*, Book II, 163.

40: "an incorporeal and endless life": Philo, "On The World," Section 3.

41: The story of Jesus and the Sadducees: Mark 12: 18–25.

46: "Why have you done this harsh thing to us?": Joshua 7:25.

46: "*Today* you are dealt with harshly": Semahot 2:9.

47: "respect for the living precedes respect for the dead": Semahot 11:6.

47: a story about Rabbi Akiva: Semahot 8:11.

48: tractate of Berakhot: Berakhot 18b.

52: the many rabbis gathered by his bedside, the Talmud relates: Ketubot 104a.

57: In Genesis Rabba: Genesis Rabba 96:5.

57: "And ye have defiled my land": Jeremiah 2:7.

57: "He will make expiation": Deuteronomy 32:43.

57: The sentiment expressed by Yohanan bar Nafha: Berakhot 34b.

58: "Neither has the eye seen": Isaiah 64:3.

58: "This world is like a vestibule": Pirkey Avot 4:16.

59: he is credited by a midrash: Ketubot 77b.

59: Another, longer midrash: Yalkut Shim'oni, Bereshit 2:20.

61: the poor scholar Raba bar Avuha: Bava Metsiya 114b.

62: "the glory of the celestial body is one thing": I Corinthians 15:40.

62: a story in Kohelet Rabba: Kohelet Rabba 3:11.

63: a tale in the Gemara's tractate of Pesahim: Pesahim 50a.

63: The Babylonian sage Rav: Berakhot 17b.

64: "A man will not doubt that he is immortal": Plotinus, Fourth Ennead, Book 7, 10.

64: "For now we see through a glass darkly": I Corinthians 13:12.

65: "When we were upon earth": *De Principiis,* Book II, 11:6.

65: The Gemara's tractate of Hagigah states: Hagigah 16a.

67: The Mishnaic sage Eleazar ha-Kappar: Pirkey Avot 4:29.

68: An originally Talmudic-period story about Rabbi Akiva: Kalla Rabati 2. A fuller form of the story is found in the probably tenth-century Midrash Aseret ha-Dibrot, Part 7.

68: In the Gemara's tractate of Eruvin: Eruvin 19a.

69: And in the tractate of Bava Batra: Bava Batra 74a.

69: "the doom of fire": Tertullian, Apology, 1:18.

69: Akiva is credited: Mishnah of Eduyot 2:10.

69: Shim'on ben Lakish, punning on the verse: Hagigah 27a.

69: "Your brow is like the curve of a pomegranate": Songs of Songs 4:3.

70: The tractate of Rosh Hashanah: Rosh Hashanah 16b–17a.

70: "And I will bring the third part": Zachariah 13: 8–9.

74: a passage from Tertullian: *De Spectaculis*, 30.

75: another tale about Akiva: Genesis Rabba 11:5.

77: The prophet Joel's description: Joel 4:2.

77: "The dead outside the land": Ketubot 111a.

81: A story in Sanhedrin: Sanhedrin 90b–91a.

82: This view is echoed in Genesis Rabba: Genesis Rabba 95:1.

82: When asked, according to the Talmud: Sanhedrin 90b.

83: The second set of questions is answered by Ulla: Sanhedrin 91b.

83: "Being taken in by the land": Ketubot 111a.

84: "If Bilam does not enter": Sanhedrin 105a.

84: Yehoshua's greater tolerance of non-Jews: Berakhot 7a.

84: "His mercy is on all His creatures": Psalms 145:9

84: "The wicked shall return to Sh'eol": Psalms 9:18.

85: "And strangers shall stand and feed your flocks": Isaiah 61:5.

86: This is the Talmudic tractate of Nidah: Nidah 61b.

86: "Free among the dead": Psalms 88:5.

91: Sa'adia begins his discussion: *The Book of Beliefs and Opinions,* Chapter 7.

94: "The only source of eternal life is knowledge": *Guide for the Perplexed,* Part III, Chapter 27.

95: "When the intellect comprehends a thing": *Guide for the Perplexed,* Part I, Chapter 48.

96: "Sa'adia, for example, describes a belief": *The Book of Beliefs and Opinions,* Chapter 6, part 7.

97: a medieval text on the subject . . . *Masekhet Hibbut ha-Kever:* in Adolph Jellinek's *Beth ha-Midrasch,* I, 150–52.

97: "There are those calling themselves Jews": *The Book of Beliefs and Opinions,* Chapter 6, part 8.

99: In one passage, the *Bahir* asks the ancient question: *Sefer ha-Bahir,* 195.

99: "He commanded His word to the thousandth generation": Psalms 105:8.

100: He does this while writing about the story of Judah: Genesis 38: 8–9.

103: "He made all the souls": Zohar II, 96b.

104: the old man of Mishpatim: Zohar II, 95a–110b.

107: According to one: *Shivhey ha-Ari,* p. 14, online edition of the Ryzman Hebrew Books series (HebrewBooks.org).

108: Another story about Luria: ibid., p. 12.

108: Hutzpit the Interpreter's *nefesh:* A "genealogy" of Hutzpit's soul is given by Luria's disciple Hayyim Vital in his *Sha'ar ha-Gilgulim,* introductory remark 36.

110: "placed the Jew in an ineluctable entanglement of transmigrations": Gershom Scholem, *On the Mystical Shape of the Godhead,* p. 241.

111: The Safed businessman Ya'akov Abulafia: *Shivhey ha-Ari,* pp. 17–18.

111: "the corners of your heads": Leviticus 19:9.

111: Another time, in the middle of teaching a lesson: *Shivhey ha-Ari,* p. 9.

112: the Koran: Sura 4 (al-Nisa), 145.

113: *Masekhet Gehinnom:* The complete text can be found in *Beth Hamidrasch,* vol. I, pp. 145–47.

114: In his *Sefer ha-Hasidim: Sefer ha-Hasidim,* 46.

114: The tiniest infraction: See, for example, *Ma'aseh Nora mi-Aniyat Amen* in Yosef Shabtai Farhi's anthology of pietistic Jewish tales *Osey Fele.*

114: In a near-death vision of the next world: As related in *Homer ha-Din* in Mordecai ben Yehezkel, *Sefer ha-Ma'asiyot,* Vol. V, pp. 302–7.

116: Karo was reassured by his *maggid*: The *maggid*'s description of Karo's reception in Heaven is found in Karo's *Maggid Meysharim*, in the diary entry for 22 Adar Alef, 1538.

117: Karo's *maggid* also explained to him: *Maggid Meysharim*, diary entry for 14 Tevet, 1538.

117: the tradition that the second-century Rabbi Meir owned a Torah scroll: Genesis Rabba, 9.

119: In a typical one, he beholds a sinner: *Mahberot Immanuel,* ed. A. N. Haberman, p. 803.

120: "its footstool scintillant with light": ibid., p. 835.

120: "a beacon for all who seek in darkness": ibid, p. 316.

121: Nahmanides, for example, thought: *Torat ha-Adam,* 77b–80a.

122: a sequence of nineteen poems: *Grand Things to Write a Poem On,* pp. 64–83.

130: A fresh grave, Semahot instructs us: Semahot, 8:1.

131: Mourners, Maimonides writes there: *Hilkhot Avel,* 14:23–24.

131: In commenting on Semahot's permission: ibid., 11:8.

132: he disagrees with Maimonides: *Torat ha-Adam,* 27b.

132: "Throughout the first three days": *Hilkhot Avel,* 13:12.

133: "A person should not go to too great lengths": ibid., 13:11.

133: "Weep ye not for the dead": Jeremiah 22:10.

133: Hanagid's verse letter to his son: *Grand Things,* pp. 84–85.

138: One of Sholem Aleichem's "Railroad Stories": "The Tenth Man" in *Tevye the Dairyman and the Railroad Stories,* translated and with an introduction by Hillel Halkin, pp. 274–79.

141: In the tractate of Berakhot: Berakhot 3a.

141: In Sota: Sota 49a.

141: In the midrash on the letter *zayin*: Jellinek, *Beth Hamidrasch,* III, pp. 27–28.

142: "On that day": *Haggai* 2:23.

143: the Polish rabbi Moshe Isserles speaks of the prayer: *Shulhan Arukh, Yoreh De'ah,* 376.

144: Isserles writes pointedly: ibid.

148: a phrase from Jeremiah: Jeremiah 2:20.

150: "The custom among Jews," writes Maimonides: *Hilkhot Avel* 4:1.

150: according to Nahmanides: *Torat ha-Adam* 17a.

153: the verse in which the dying Jacob: Genesis 47:29.

153: Genesis Rabba comments: Genesis Rabba 96:5.

154: he writes that the soul stays by the body: *Ma'avar Yabok, S'fat Emet,* 25.

157: "Eulogizing the dead is of great value": ibid., 19.

159: The words of the first-century Akavya ben Mehalalel: Pirkey Avot 3:1.

160: Berakhiah seeks to give: *Ma'avar Yabok: Siftey Renanot* 15.

161: "The Rock, His work is perfect": Deuteronomy 32:4.

165: Not long ago I read an essay: Joyce Slochower, "The Therapeutic Function of Shivah," in *Jewish Insights on Death and Mourning,* ed. Jack Riemer.

166: "No one at a shiva," writes Maimonides: *Hilkhot Avel,*13:3.

166: "The Art of Making A Shivah Call": Ron Wolfson in Riemer, *Jewish Insights on Death and Mourning.*

168: There is a well-known tale: "Three Gifts," in *The I. L. Peretz Reader,* ed. Ruth Wisse, pp. 222–29.

168: In a story attributed: *Sefer ha-Ma'asiyot* II, pp. 149–52.

169: according to Berakhiah: *Ma'avar Yabok, S'fat Emet,* 1.

170: Another of Sholem Aleichem's "Railroad Stories": "Elul," in Sholem Aleichem, *Tevye the Dairyman,* pp. 177–83.

172: "Lo, I am gathered unto my people": Genesis 49:29.

172: A Hasidic story: *Sefer ha-Ma'asiyot* V, pp. 308–14.

182: the ninth-century Midrash Tanhuma: Tanhuma Ha'azinu 1.

183: the Hebrew writer David Frischmann recounts: *Hazkarat Neshamot, Kol Kitvey David Frischmann,* pp. 95–104.

187: a book published in 1947: the Orthodox Rosh Hashanah almanac *Nerot Shabbat.*

187: In it was this *yizkor* written by him: Katznelson's *yizkor* first appeared in the left-wing periodical *Kuntres,* no. 29, 1920.

192: So begins a poem: Dudi Ben-Ami, *Even ve'Ahavot Aherot, 2010.*

194: "walking, still walking": David Grossman, *Nofel Mi'hutz la-Z'man,* pp. 114–15.

201: "quivering with terror" before the specter of death: Franz Rosenzweig, *The Star of Redemption,* translated by William Hallo, p. 3.

201: "quite beyond the imagination": ibid., p. 80.

202: a series of interviews about the afterlife: Blu Greenberg, "Is There Life after Death?" in Riemer, *Jewish Insights on Death and Mourning*.

204: "When a person goes to his eternal home": Ta'anit 11a. Raphaell's discussion is on p. 376 of *Jewish Views of the Afterlife*.

204: "Individuals who have practiced": Raphaell, *Jewish Views of the Afterlife*, p. 373.

205: Gehenna, he writes, "provides a concentrated opportunity": ibid., pp. 385–86.

209: a long midrash about the death of Moses: *Yalkut Shim'oni*, Devarim 31.

213: And He wept and said: Psalms 94, 16.

214: In Franz Rosenzweig's words: *The Star of Redemption*, p. 3.